D0182647

The Complete Piano Player

by **Kenneth Baker**

OMNIBUS PRESS

Part Two

Part Three

786.3
1095446

HOW TO SIT CORRECTLY

It is important to sit correctly at the piano. The more comfortable you are, the easier it is to play. Sit as shown here and you will always feel comfortable and relaxed.

Sit facing the middle of the instrument, your feet opposite the pedals. Sit upright. Adjust your seat so that your arms are level with the keyboard–or sloping down slightly towards it.

POSITION OF THE HANDS

Support your hands from the wrists. Curve your fingers slightly as if you were grasping lightly an imaginary ball.

With the tips of your fingers cover five adjacent notes in each hand. This is the normal Five-Finger Playing Position. It is also the hand's most relaxed state. After all fingering and hand changes during a piece, you should return to this position.

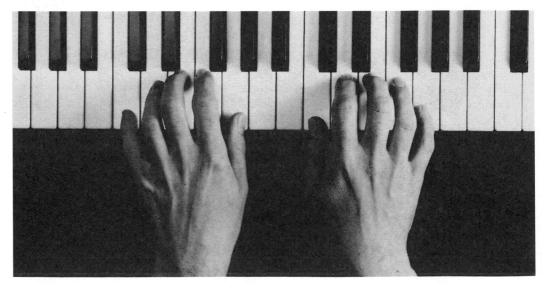

THE PIANO KEYBOARD

2

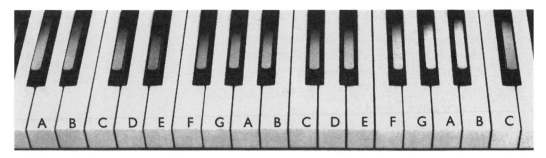

There are only seven letter names used in music: A B C D E F G.
These seven letter names repeat over and over again on the keyboard.

The black keys are arranged in groups of twos and threes.

HOW TO LEARN THE WHITE KEYS: C, D & E

Use the black keys to locate the white keys.
For example, 'D' lies between two black keys.

To the left of D lies C.
To the right of D lies E:

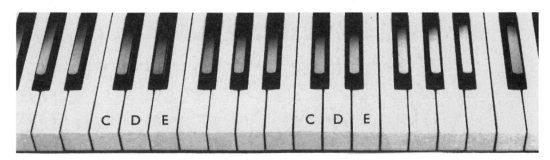

HOW TO LEARN THE WHITE KEYS: F, G, A & B

Use the groups of three black keys to
locate F, G, A and B (the remaining four
letters of the musical alphabet):

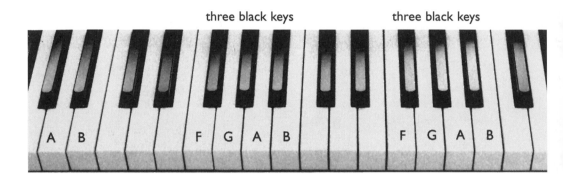

Find all the F's, G's, A's and B's on your
piano.
Play each note in turn and name it.

HOW TO LEARN THE WHITE KEYS: C to B

Play every 'set' of white notes, beginning
with C and ending on B. Play in all
positions on the piano. Do this several
times, naming the notes as you play
them.

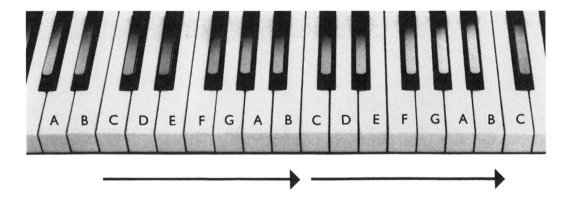

**You now know all the white notes and
their names.**

AN IMPORTANT NOTE: MIDDLE C

3

One of the most important notes on the piano is Middle C. This is the C nearest the middle of the instrument, directly opposite the manufacturer's name, as you sit at the piano.

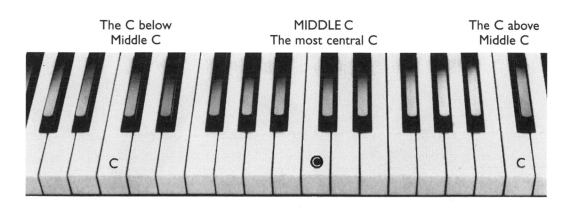

The C below Middle C   MIDDLE C The most central C   The C above Middle C

Look at the illustration above. From it, you will see that:

The C to the left of Middle C is called 'The C below middle C.'

The C to the right of middle C is called 'The C above middle C.' You should, at this stage, be able to find these three C's right away. Learn to find them this easy way:

● Play Middle C with the right hand (any finger will do).
● Play Middle C with the left hand.
● Play The C below Middle C with the left hand.
● Play The C above Middle C with the right hand.
● Finally: play Middle C again with one of the fingers of each hand.

You now know where to find Middle C and the C's immediately above and below it.

FINGER NUMBERS

4

To make learning easy, the fingers of both hands are given numbers:

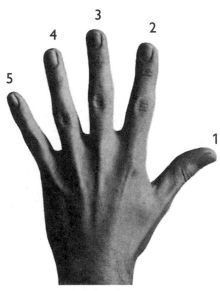

left hand

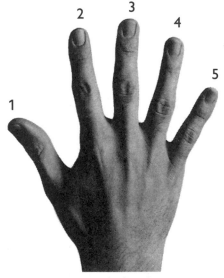

right hand

You will see that the thumb counts as finger Number 1.

To familiarise you with the finger numbers of the right hand, we are going to play the great jazz number: *When The Saints Go Marching In.*

Before you start to play, cover the five notes from Middle C to G above it with the five fingers of your right hand, like this:

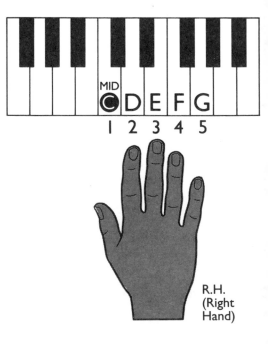

R.H.
(Right
Hand)

Now play each note with the fingers shown below. To help you play in time, tap your foot to the music. The little diagrams below the finger numbers ♪ show you when to tap.

Notice that every so often the tune 'stays still,' while you go on tapping your foot. Remember to hold the note down during this time.

WHEN THE SAINTS GO MARCHING IN
Traditional

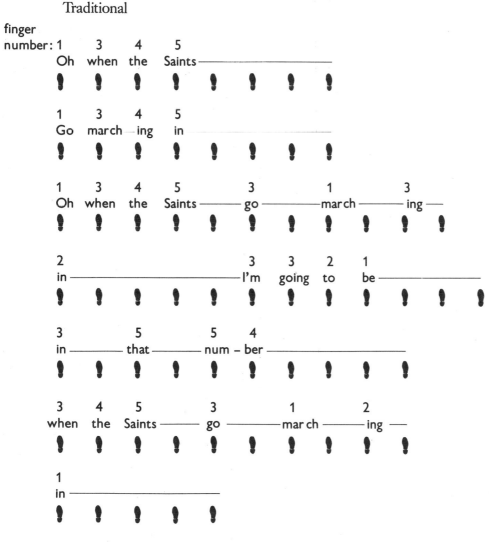

You now know the finger numbers of the right hand.

HOW TO PLAY LEGATO

5

Legato means 'joined up'. When you play legato, your playing sounds smooth and connected.

To get this smooth and connected effect, as each new note is played you release the preceding note. In other words: one finger exactly replaces another. The result is a continuous, unbroken flow of sound. This is true legato playing.

Always play legato unless the music is marked otherwise.

In your efforts to play legato, never let one sound overlap the next. If you do, you may get an ugly sound mixture. Your ear will tell you when you are playing legato. Remember:

● No gaps.
● No overlaps.

Now play *When The Saints Go Marching In* again. Are you playing smoothly? Do all the notes join up? If so, you are playing legato.

LEFT HAND FINGER NUMBERS

You are now going to learn the left hand finger numbers by playing the traditional tune: *Banks Of The Ohio.*

Before you start to play, cover the five notes from C below Middle C to G with the five fingers of your left hand:

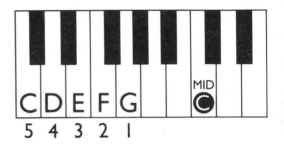

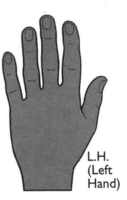

L.H.
(Left
Hand)

Now, play each note according to the finger numbers given.

Tap your foot to keep time, as before…

Remember: play legato

BANKS OF THE OHIO
Traditional

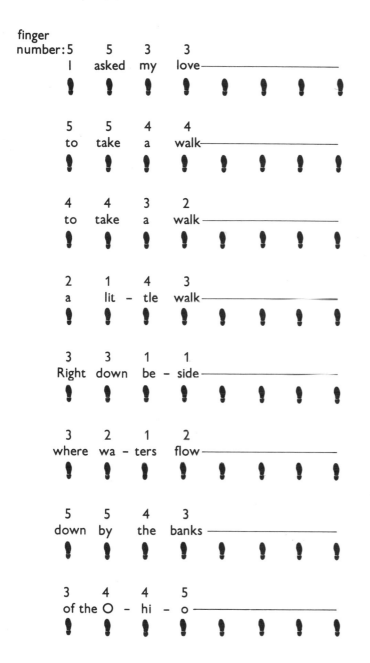

finger
number:
5	5	3	3
I	asked	my	love————————————

5	5	4	4
to	take	a	walk————————————

4	4	3	2
to	take	a	walk————————————

2	1	4	3
a	lit – tle	walk————————————	

3	3	1	1
Right	down	be – side————————————	

3	2	1	2
where	wa – ters	flow————————————	

5	5	4	3
down	by	the	banks ————————————

3	4	4	5
of the O – hi – o ————————————			

You now know the finger numbers of the left hand.

HOW NOTES ARE WRITTEN

6

Musical notes are written on groups of
five lines called 'staves':

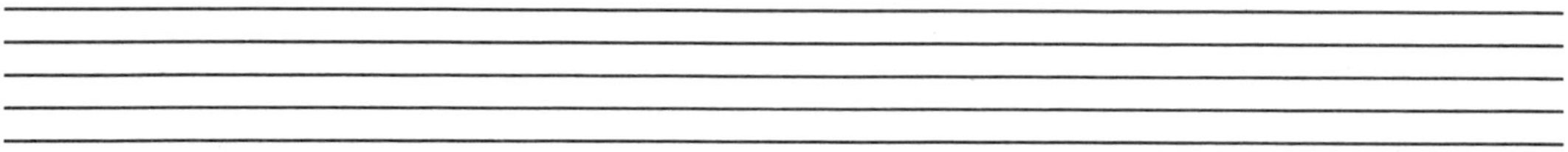

A stave

The notes may be written on any 'line':

or in any 'space' between lines:

this counts as a 'space'

this counts as a 'space'

The piano needs two staves: one for the
top half of the instrument:

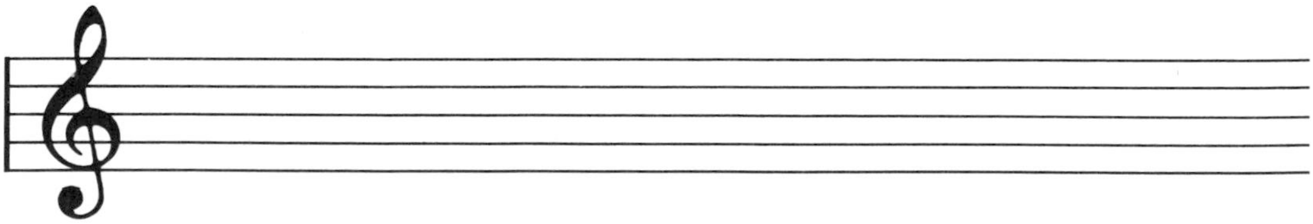

This sign is called the 'Treble Clef'

and one for the bottom half:

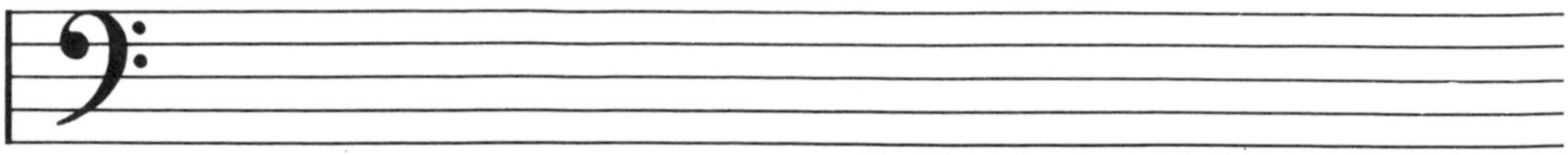

This sign is called the 'Bass Clef'

The two staves are joined together by a 'brace':

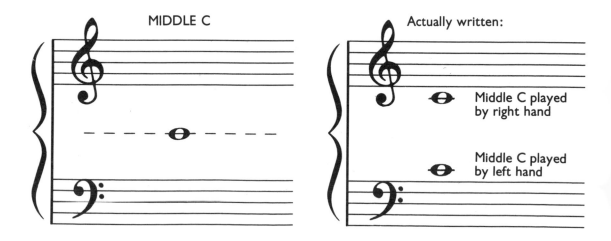

The notes on the upper stave (indicated by the Treble Clef) are usually played by the right hand.

The notes on the lower stave (indicated by the Bass Clef) are usually played by the left hand.

Middle C falls on a line exactly between the two staves.

MIDDLE C

Actually written:

Middle C played by right hand

Middle C played by left hand

The Middle C line is never drawn in its entirety since that would cause confusion with the other lines. A partial line is all that is needed:

MIDDLE C

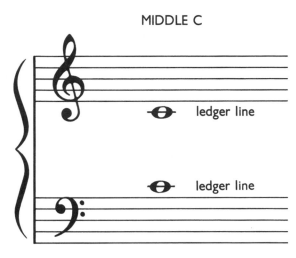

Such partial lines are called 'ledger lines.'

Now let's see how your first five notes for right hand are written:

Cover the five notes Middle C to G with the fingers of your right hand:

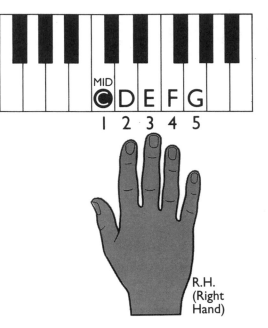

You used these notes in *When The Saints Go Marching In*, on page 11.

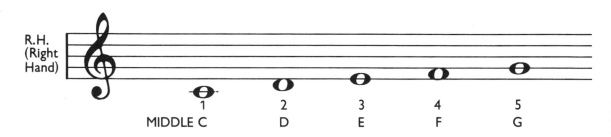

Learn these notes now.

Cover the five notes with the correct fingers of your right hand and play the next tune: *I Know Where I'm Going*:

16

I KNOW WHERE I'M GOING

Words & Music: Herbert Hughes

7

You now know your first five right hand notes and how they are written.

Let's learn the first five left hand notes. Start at Middle C and work down the keyboard (i.e. to the left). These are the five notes:

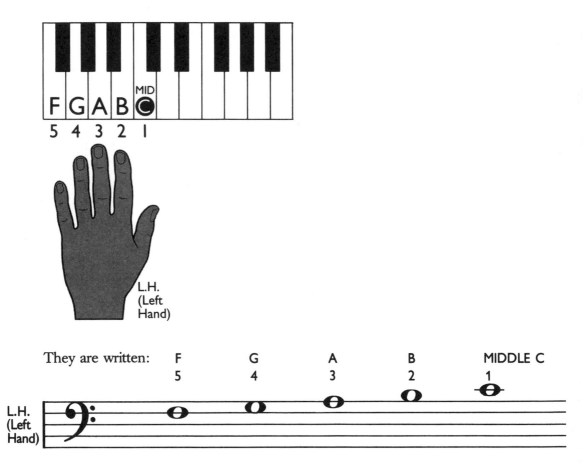

They are written:

	F	G	A	B	MIDDLE C
	5	4	3	2	1

L.H. (Left Hand)

Learn these notes now.

Cover the notes with the correct fingers of your left hand and play your next tune:
Rivers Of Babylon.

RIVERS OF BABYLON

Words & Music: Farian, Reyam, Dowe and McMaughton

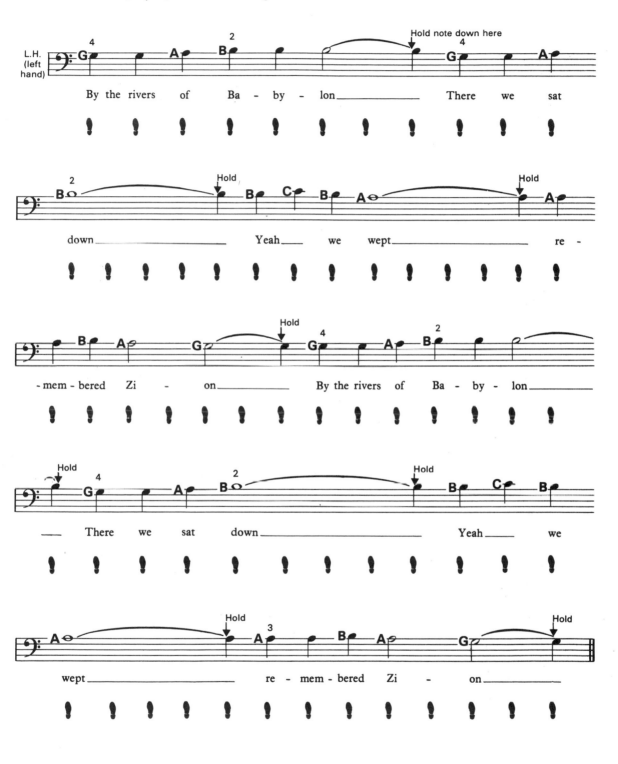

You now know nine important notes and how they are written:

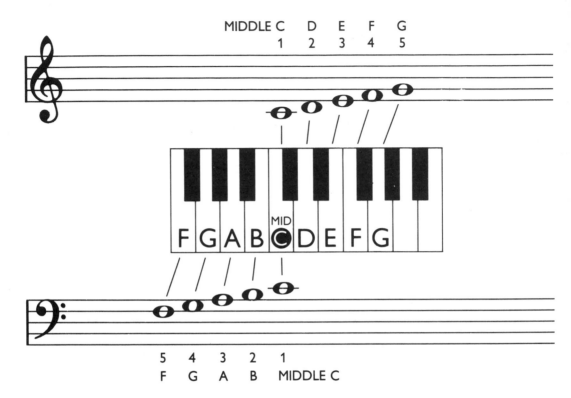

These nine notes are all that are needed to play all the songs in this book.

After this, new notes will be added gradually. Keyboard charts will be given to illustrate new notes as they occur.

The cardboard chart included with this book fits over the piano keyboard and may be used for reference. In addition, in this book, 'letter names' have been written against the notes. But, you **should memorise all new notes as soon as possible.**

MUSICAL TIMING AND THE BEAT

8

The 'Beat' is the name given to the rhythmic pulse felt behind most music.

When you were tapping your foot to *When The Saints Go Marching In, Banks Of The Ohio,* and *Rivers Of Babylon,* you were tapping out the beat. In most tunes there is a series of natural 'accents', which recur regularly every few beats. A line called a 'bar line' is drawn in front of every one of these natural accents. These lines divide the music into 'bars' or 'measures'.

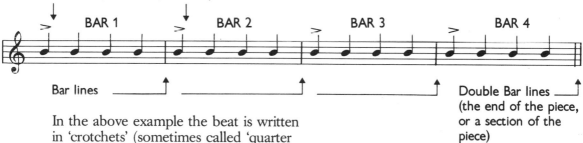

Accents (not usually marked)

BAR 1   BAR 2   BAR 3   BAR 4

Bar lines

Double Bar lines (the end of the piece, or a section of the piece)

In the above example the beat is written in 'crotchets' (sometimes called 'quarter notes'):

(Note that the 'tails' or 'stems' may be written up or down).

Look at the above example again, and you will see that there are four crotchets (quarter notes) to the bar. This is indicated at the beginning of the piece like this:

Time Signature

The above pair of numbers is called the 'time signature'. In every time signature there is:
An 'upper figure': this shows how many beats there are in the bar (four in our example).

A 'lower figure': this shows how the beats are written. In our example the lower figure 4 means that the beats are written as crotchets ("quarter" notes).

21

Here is another example:

This time, the upper figure tells you that there are three beats to the bar. The lower figure is still 4, so there are: Three crotchets (quarter notes) to the bar.

The next song you are going to learn is *This Ole House.* It is written entirely in crotchets:

Tap your foot on each crotchet – this will help keep you in time.

You will be using the same five right hand notes as before:

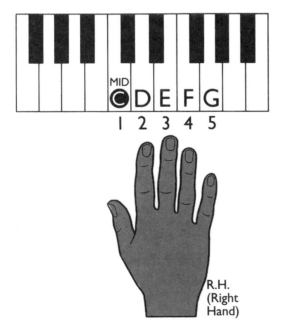

Cover these notes before you start to play. Your first note is E, played by the 3rd finger.

Notice that there are four crotchets in each bar, and the tune starts on the third beat of the bar.

THIS OLE HOUSE

Words & Music by: Stuart Hamblen

You now know about crotchets (quarter notes).

DEVELOPING YOUR SENSE OF RHYTHM

9

The melody notes of *This Ole House* corresponded with the crotchet beat exactly. But usually a melody includes a number of notes of longer duration.

This is how some of these longer time notes are written:

Name of note	How written				Duration
Minim (half note)	♩ =	♩	♩		Lasts for two (crotchet) beats
Dotted minim (dotted half note)	♩. =	♩	♩	♩	Lasts for three (crotchet) beats
Semibreve (whole note)	𝅝 =	♩	♩	♩ ♩	Lasts for four (crotchet) beats.

To get you used to these different time notes, I want you to play now some rhythm exercises. They are written entirely on Middle C.

The first rhythm exercise is for the right hand. It features 'crotchets', 'minims', 'dotted minims' and 'semibreves'.
In each bar, there are four crotchets (or their equivalent).
Choose a suitable speed (not too fast), and maintain the same speed throughout. Tap your foot once on every crotchet beat.

RHYTHM EXERCISE 1

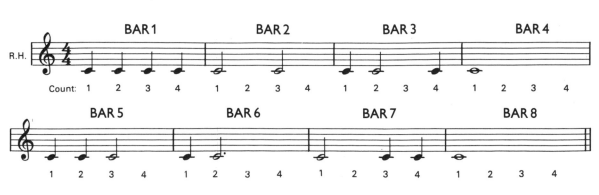

24

Bar 1 Play Middle C on beats 1, 2, 3 and 4.

Bar 2 Play C on beat 1 and let the sound continue while you count and tap beat 2. Play C on beat 3 and let the sound continue while you count and tap beat 4.

Bar 3 Play C on beat 1.
Play C on beat 2 and let the sound continue while you count and tap beat 3.
Play C on beat 4.

Bar 4 Play C on beat 1 and let the sound continue while you count and tap beats 2, 3 and 4.

Continue similarly to bar 8.

Did you keep your speed constant?

Now another rhythm exercise, this time for the left hand. Again you will be using Middle C only.

This exercise is in $\frac{3}{4}$ Time, in other words there are three crotchets (or their equivalent) to the bar.

RHYTHM EXERCISE 2

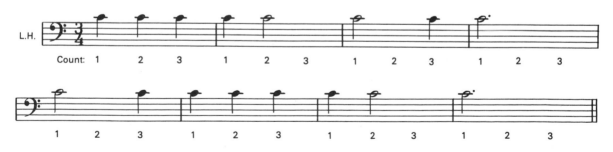

Did you keep your speed constant?

You now know about:
1 beat notes ♩ Crotchets (quarter notes)
2 beat notes ♩ Minims (half notes)

3 beat notes ♩. Dotted minims (dotted half notes)
4 beat notes o Semibreves (whole notes)

MORE ABOUT RHYTHM

From now on you will be called upon to put your knowledge of rhythm to work. The popular tunes you are going to learn will use all four kinds of notes: crotchets, minims, dotted minims and semibreves. Check that you know them thoroughly.

You are first going to play *White Rose Of Athens* for the right hand. As usual before you start to play, cover the notes Middle C to G with the five fingers of your right hand.

The tune starts on Middle C played with the thumb. There are four crotchets (or their equivalent) to the bar.

Remember to play legato

WHITE ROSE OF ATHENS

Music: Manos Hadjidakis. Words: Norman Newell.
Additional Words: Archie Bleyer.

NOTES REQUIRED

MID C D E F G

FINGERING 1 2 3 4 5
(RIGHT HAND)

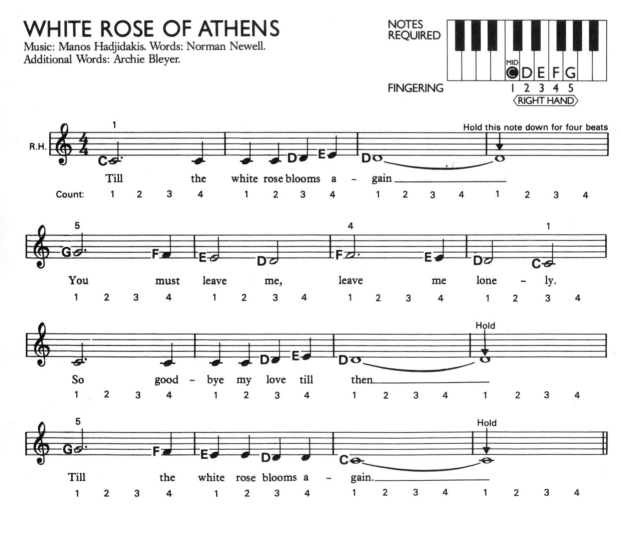

Now two famous Beatles themes, both
for left hand. Before you start to play,
cover the notes Middle C to F with the
fingers of your left hand.

The first theme starts on F with the fifth
finger and you start playing on the
second beat of the bar.

Remember to play legato.

CAN'T BUY ME LOVE / SHE LOVES YOU

Words & Music: John Lennon & Paul McCartney

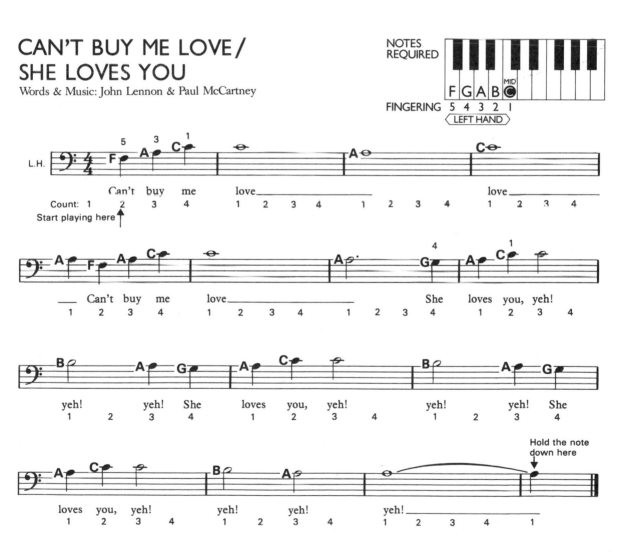

Now a Beatles tune for right hand: *Help*.

There are four crotchets to the bar. You will be using crotchets, minims, and semibreves.

Before you start to play, cover the notes Middle C to G with the five fingers of your right hand.

The tune starts on the second beat of the bar with the note E (3rd finger).

HELP
Words & Music: John Lennon and Paul McCartney

NOTES REQUIRED

FINGERING   1 2 3 4 5
(RIGHT HAND)

*This curved line concerns the singer only and is called a 'Melisma Mark' or 'Singer's Slur'. Here the singer continues the syllable '-sured' through the three notes E, D and C. Look on the next page for five more 'Singer's Slurs'.

*This curved line is a 'tie' (see page 31)
not a 'Singer's Slur'.

EXCERPT FROM A FAMOUS CLASSIC

Your next piece is the Largo from *The New World Symphony* by Dvořák.

The first part is played by your left hand; the second part is played by your right hand; the final part is played by your left hand.

Watch out for crotchets, minims and semibreves in this piece.

LARGO
(FROM THE NEW WORLD SYMPHONY)
By: Antonin Dvořák

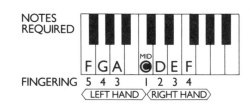

TIES

12

Let me just remind you of the names of the time notes and how long they last:

Crotchet (quarter note)	♩	1 beat
Minim (half note)	♩	2 beats
Dotted minim (dotted half note)	♩.	3 beats
Semibreve (whole note)	o	4 beats

Each of the time notes may be extended by the use of a 'Tie'. A tie is a curved line connecting two notes of the same pitch – in other words, two notes in the same position on the stave.

TIE (hold down the note)

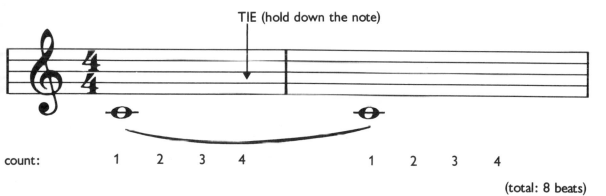

count: 1   2   3   4   1   2   3   4

(total: 8 beats)

Here you play the first Middle C and count for the second Middle C without striking the note again. Total time: 2 semibreves, or 8 crotchet beats.

A reminder:

You have already met ties in *Rivers Of Babylon, White Rose Of Athens, She Loves You,* and *Help* (see the last note E).

Now play all these pieces through again, and this time pay particular attention to the ties.

TWO MORE POPULAR TUNES WITH TIES

13

The next tune, *What Now My Love*, also features ties and is for the right hand. Before you start to play, cover the usual notes, Middle C to G, with the right hand fingers.

The tune starts on the second beat of the bar.

WHAT NOW MY LOVE

English Words: Carl Sigman. French Lyric: P Delanoe.
Music: G Becaud.

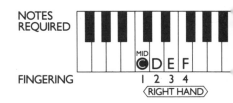

NOTES REQUIRED

FINGERING

Here is another tune which features ties.
It is for the left hand.

Before you start to play, cover Middle C
to F with the five fingers of the left hand:

This tune starts on G with the 4th finger.
There are four crotchets (or their
equivalent) per bar, and the tune starts
on beat 2:

ONE OF THOSE SONGS
(LE BAL DE MADAME DE MORTEMOUILLE)
English lyric: Will Holt. Music: Gerard Calvi

NOTES
REQUIRED

G A B C
MID

FINGERING   4 3 2 I
⟨ LEFT HAND ⟩

**Now you know about ties and how
they make the notes last longer.**

14

This is the first time that you have had to read music written on two staves. In your next piece both hands share the tune. This is why two staves are necessary. Play the piece several times and get used to reading two staves.

The left hand plays first. It starts on G with the 4th finger.

LOVE ME TENDER

Words and Music: Elvis Presley & Vera Matson

NOTES REQUIRED

G	A	B	MID C	D	E	F

FINGERING 4 3 2 1 2 3 4

‹ LEFT HAND × RIGHT HAND ›

TWO STAVES AGAIN

You will use both hands again in the next piece: *Mary's Boy Child.*
The right hand plays first. It starts on E with the 3rd finger.

MARY'S BOY CHILD
Words & Music: Jester Hairston

PHRASE MARKS

16

Curved lines over or under the notes are called: 'Phrase Marks,' or 'Slurs.' Phrase marks are not to be confused with 'ties':

Phrase mark (play legato)   Tie (hold down the note)

Unless directed otherwise, play all notes within phrase marks legato (joined up).

I'D LIKE TO TEACH THE WORLD TO SING

Words & Music: Roger Cook, Roger Greenaway, Billy Backer & Billy Davis

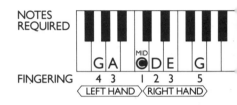

NOTES REQUIRED

FINGERING

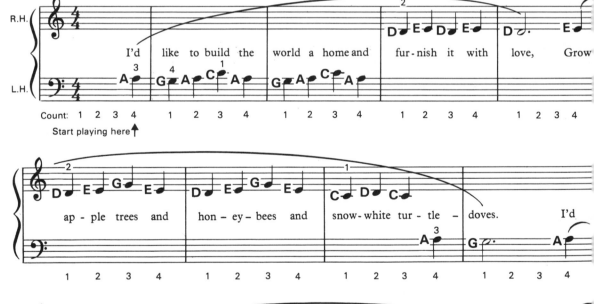

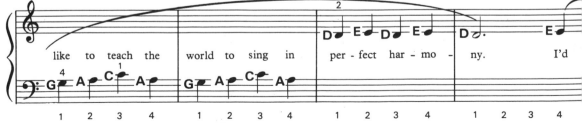

STREETS OF LONDON

Words & Music: Ralph McTell

QUAVERS

17

The next three pieces feature a new time note: the quaver.

Quavers (or eighth notes)

Quavers move twice as fast as the basic crotchet beat:

If you say the word 'and' between beat numbers, it will give you the time of the quaver. You will come across quavers in bars 10 and 11 of the famous theme from the *Choral Symphony* by Beethoven. In this and the following two pieces I have marked the places at which you should say 'and' when counting.

Theme from CHORAL SYMPHONY
By: Ludwig van Beethoven

NOTES REQUIRED

CHITTY CHITTY BANG BANG

Words & Music: Richard M. Sherman and Robert B. Sherman

STACCATO AND ACCENT

18

A dot over or under a note means that the note is to be played 'Staccato,' which means 'cut short.' Keep the wrist loose and 'peck' at the note with the finger. Staccato (cut short) is the opposite of legato (smooth and connected).

Staccato – cut the note(s) short

A dash over or under a note means hold the note for its full value, or even a fraction more.

Accent (Tenuto mark) – hold the note(s) for its full value

In the next piece make the contrast between staccato and accented notes.

OLD MACDONALD HAD A FARM
Traditional

SCARLET RIBBONS

Words by Jack Segal. Music by Evelyn Danzig.

NOTES REQUIRED

FINGERING 5 4 3 2 1 2 3 4 5
LEFT HAND ⟩⟨ RIGHT HAND

p (soft)

crescendo or cresc.
(getting louder)

mf (moderately loud)

p

Ritenuto or Rit.
(Slowing down)

*Repeat Marking. Go back to the matching sign: ‖: and play through the first 8 Bars again.

RESTS AND SILENCE

19

Silence in music is important. Silences can be dramatic, romantic, or add an air of expectancy. To indicate silence in music, signs called 'Rests' are used. Each Time Note has its own rest.

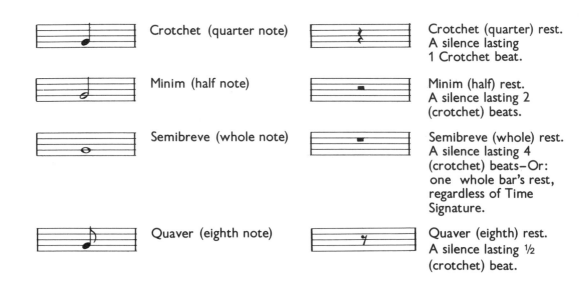

Crotchet (quarter note)

Crotchet (quarter) rest.
A silence lasting
1 Crotchet beat.

Minim (half note)

Minim (half) rest.
A silence lasting 2
(crotchet) beats.

Semibreve (whole note)

Semibreve (whole) rest.
A silence lasting 4
(crotchet) beats–Or:
one whole bar's rest,
regardless of Time
Signature.

Quaver (eighth note)

Quaver (eighth) rest.
A silence lasting ½
(crotchet) beat.

You will come across various rests in *Annie's Song* which you are going to play now. Make sure you respect these silences. The first few rests are 'arrowed' to make it easier for you.

ANNIE'S SONG
Words & Music by John Denver

NOTES REQUIRED

A C D E F G
FINGERING 3 1 2 3 4 5
LEFT HAND RIGHT HAND

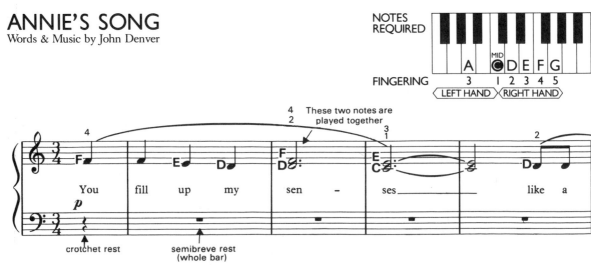

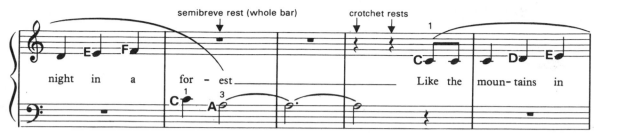

semibreve rest (whole bar)   crotchet rests

night in a for-est ____ Like the moun-tains in

These two notes (E and C) are played together

spring — time ____ Like a walk in the rain ____

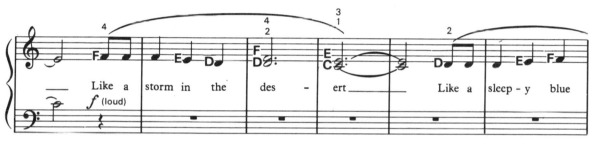

___ Like a storm in the des — ert ____ Like a sleep-y blue

f (loud)

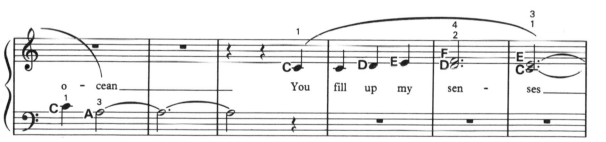

o-cean ____ You fill up my sen - ses ____

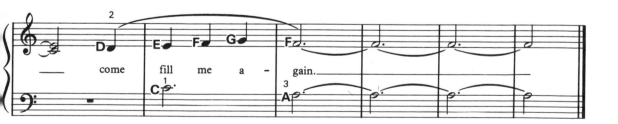

___ come fill me a - gain. ____

I have 'arrowed' the first few rests in this piece. After that I leave it to you to watch for and respect the rests.

STRANGERS IN THE NIGHT
Music: Bert Kaempfert. Words: Charles Singleton & Eddie Snyder.

two lone - ly peo - ple we were stran - gers in the night

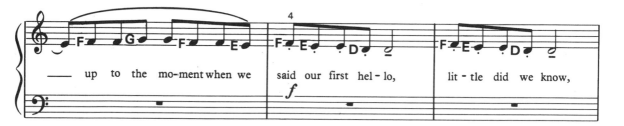

up to the mo-ment when we said our first hel - lo, lit - tle did we know,

love was just a glance a - way, a warm em-brac-ing dance a - way and ev - er since that night

we've been to - ge - ther lov - ers at first sight in love for - ev - er

It turned out so right for stran - gers in the night.

SINGIN' IN THE RAIN

Words: Arthur Freed. Music: Nacio Herb Brown

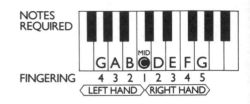

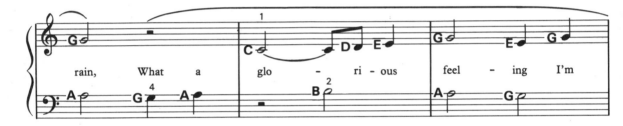

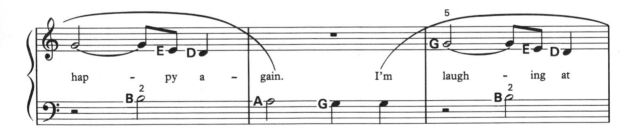

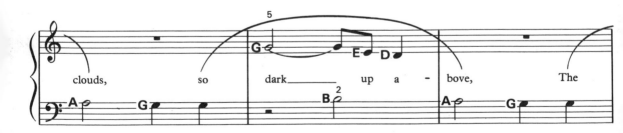

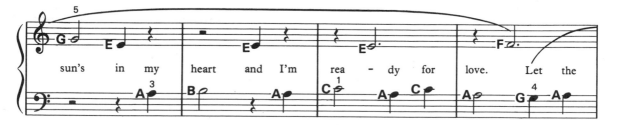

sun's in my heart and I'm rea - dy for love. Let the

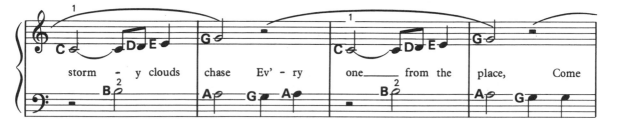

storm - y clouds chase Ev' - ry one___ from the place, Come

on___ with the rain, I've a smile___ on my face. I'll

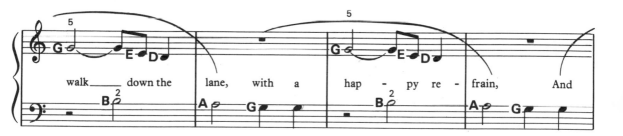

walk___ down the lane, with a hap - py re - frain, And

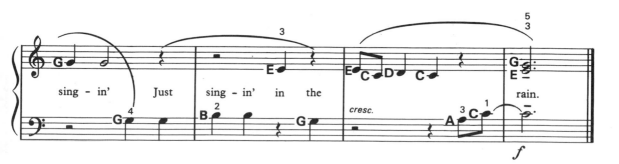

sing - in' Just sing - in' in the rain.

LAST WORD

Congratulations on completing Part One of 'The Complete Piano Player.'

In Part Two you will be:
- Learning new notes
- Finding out more about 'fingering'
- Using sharps and flats
- Understanding something about 'keys'
- Discovering new piano techniques.

In the meantime your last song in this Part is: *Super Trouper*

SUPER TROUPER
Words & Music by Benny Andersson and Bjorn Ulvaeus

The Complete Piano Player

by **Kenneth Baker**

NEW NOTES

You start this book by learning these new notes:

A, B, C right hand
E left hand

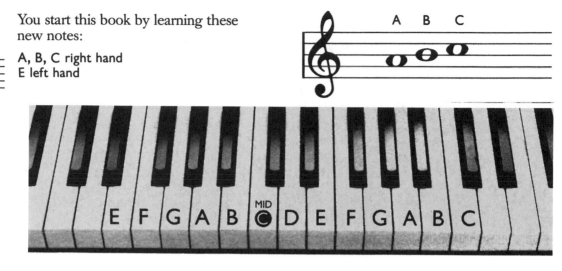

HOW TO FINGER THE NEW NOTES

The new notes illustrated above are beyond the range of your original five-fingered hand positions:

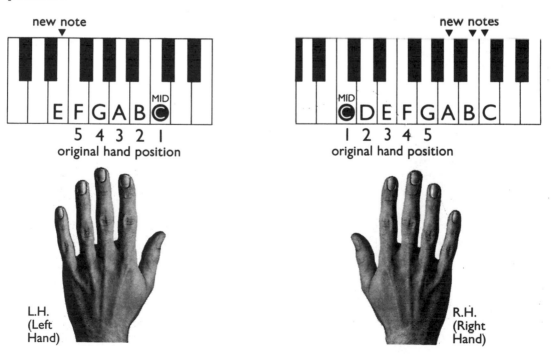

When a single new note is required, extend your hand to play it, then return to your original five finger hand position:

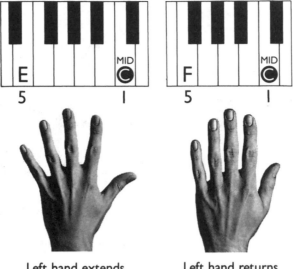

Left hand extends
to play note E

Left hand returns
to original five-finger
position.

When several new notes are to be played consecutively take up a new five-finger position covering the new notes:

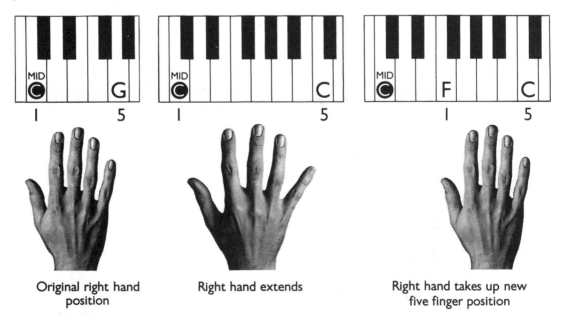

Original right hand
position

Right hand extends

Right hand takes up new
five finger position

I have indicated examples of both the above situations in the three pieces which follow: *Sailing, My Own True Love,* and *Wooden Heart.*

Note: From now on letter names will appear alongside new notes only.

SAILING
Words & Music: Gavin Sutherland

Remember: watch out for changes of hand positions in this and the next two pieces.

MY OWN TRUE LOVE
(TARA'S THEME)
Words: Mack David. Music: Max Steiner.

Always change hand positions smoothly

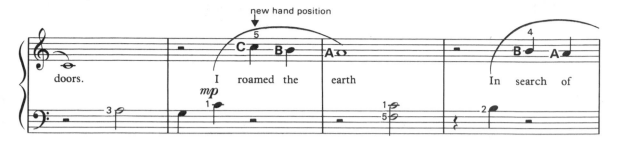

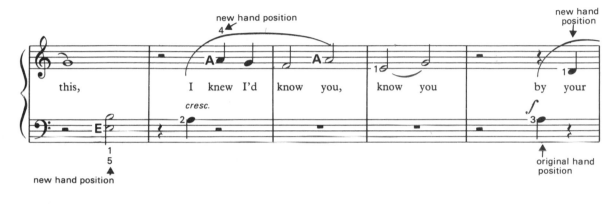

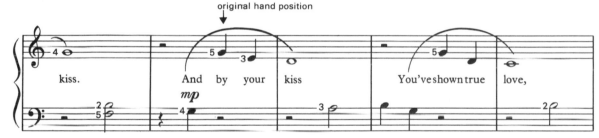

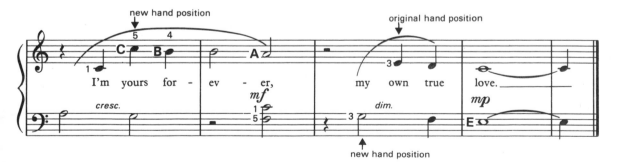

WOODEN HEART

Words & Music by Fred Wise, Ben Weisman,
Kay Twomey and Berthold Kaempfert.

Change hand positions smoothly

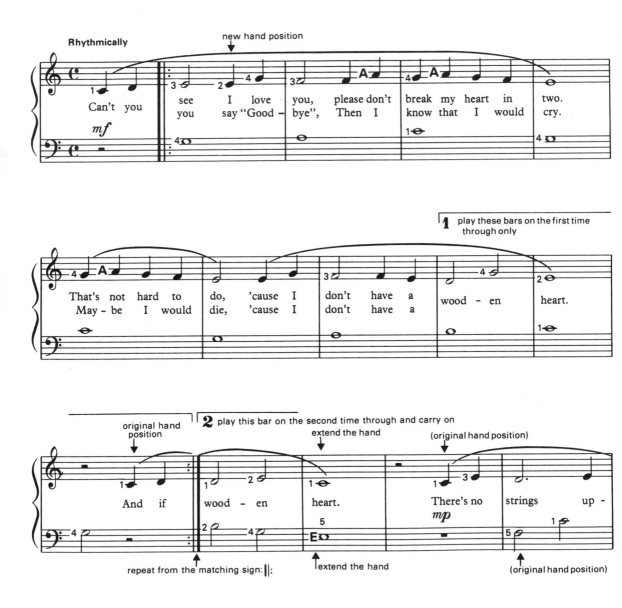

new hand position

Rhythmically

mf

Can't you | see I love you, please don't break my heart in two.
 | you say "Good - bye", Then I know that I would cry.

1 play these bars on the first time through only

That's not hard to do, 'cause I don't have a wood - en heart.
May - be I would die, 'cause I don't have a

original hand position

2 play this bar on the second time through and carry on

extend the hand

(original hand position)

And if wood - en heart. There's no strings up -

mp

repeat from the matching sign: ‖:   extend the hand   (original hand position)

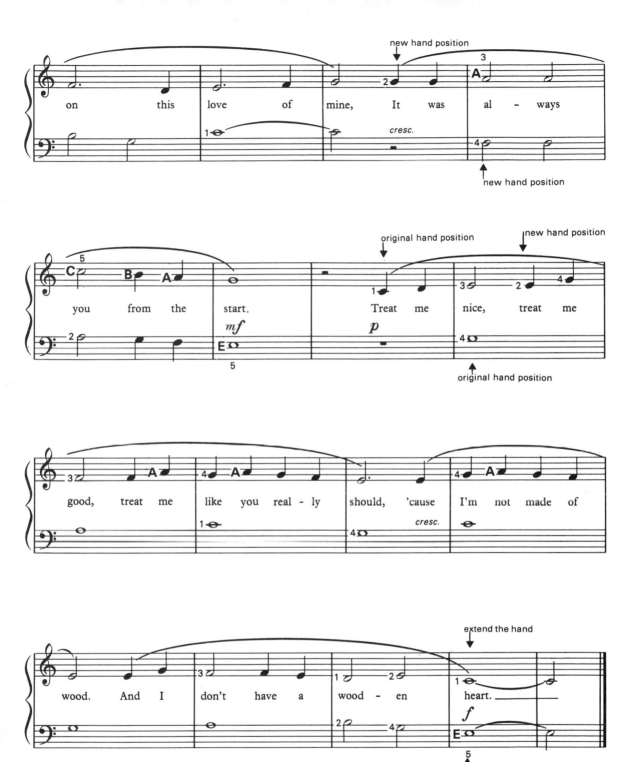

From now on I leave it to you to watch out for hand extensions and changes of hand position. Follow the printed fingering carefully and you can't go wrong.

DANNY BOY
Words: Fred E. Weatherly. Music: Traditional Irish Melody

With expression

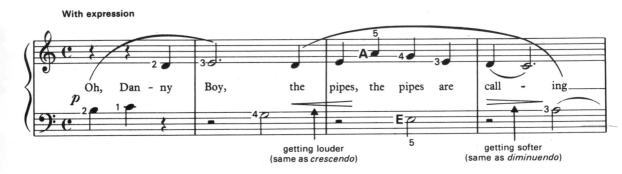

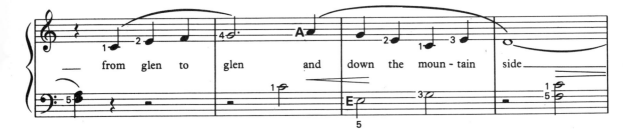

It's you, it's you must go and I must bide.

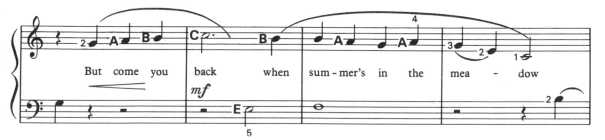

But come you back when sum-mer's in the mea-dow

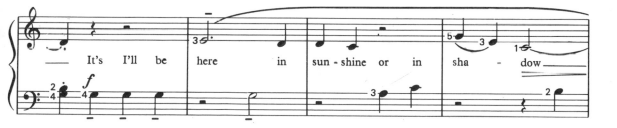

Or when the val-ley's hushed and white with snow

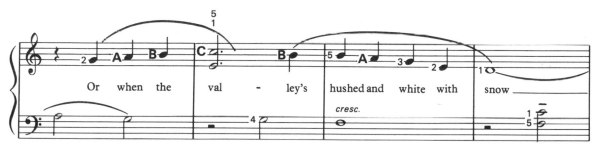

It's I'll be here in sun-shine or in sha-dow

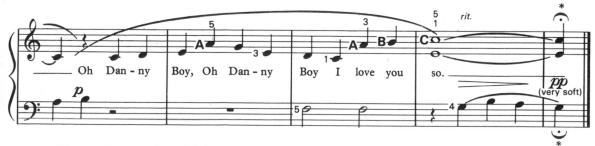

Oh Dan-ny Boy, Oh Dan-ny Boy I love you so.

*Pause (Fermata). Hold the note(s)
longer than written (at the discretion of
the player).

SHARPS AND NATURALS

2

This sign is called a sharp: ♯ Whenever you see a sharp written against a note, it means that you must play the nearest available key to the right of that note. This key may be **black or white.**

You continue to play the sharp throughout the bar, but it is automatically cancelled at the next bar.

Another way of cancelling a sharp is by writing a 'natural' sign against the note. The natural sign is written like this: ♮ For an example of the use of a natural sign, see bar 15 of *Puff The Magic Dragon*.

The most commonly used sharp is:

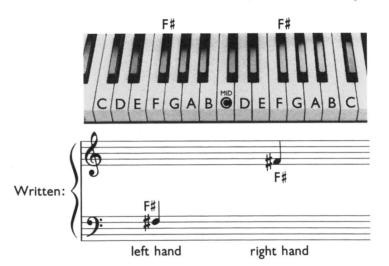

Written:

left hand   right hand

EXAMPLES OF OTHER SHARPS

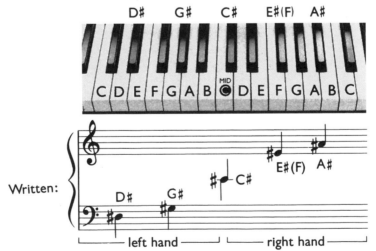

Written:

left hand — right hand

Notice that E♯ and F are exactly the same note. Sometimes it is more convenient to call F 'E♯'

60

PUFF (THE MAGIC DRAGON)

Words & Music by: Peter Yarrow and Leonard Lipton

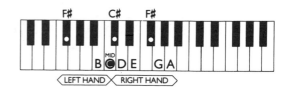

Watch out for 'sharp' notes in this piece. Remember to return to 'natural' notes.

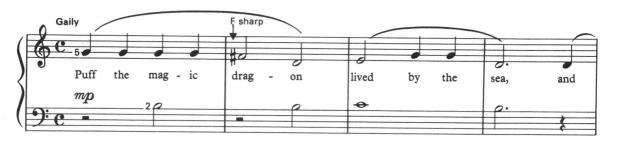

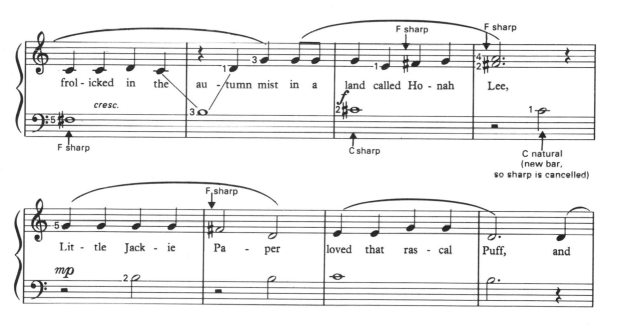

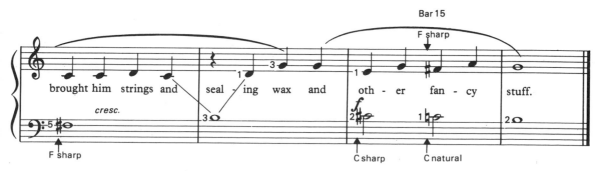

METRONOME MARKS

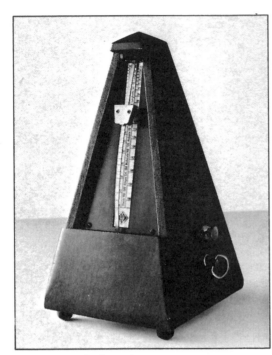

clockwork metronome

electronic metronome

A metronome is an instrument which indicates the speed of a piece of music.

The metronome mark: ♩ = 176 at the beginning of the next piece means that there are to be 176 Crotchets (quarter notes) a minute (rather fast).
Set the pendulum to 176 and the instrument will "tick" at the correct speed. Don't leave the metronome running during your piece. Once you have the "feel" of the correct speed, switch off.

CHORD SYMBOLS

From now on chord symbols will be included in all pieces. These symbols are intended for other instrumentalists, such as guitarists, who may wish to accompany you.

LAUGHING SAMBA
Words: Benny Meroff & Anne Spear.
Music: Vincent Rizzo & George Johnson.

Brightly ♩ = 176

Fun – ny   lit – tle   "Song – a",   some-thing like   a   Con – ga,
Ev' – ry   one can   do   it,   there is   noth – ing   to   it,

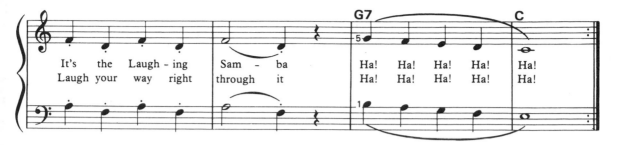

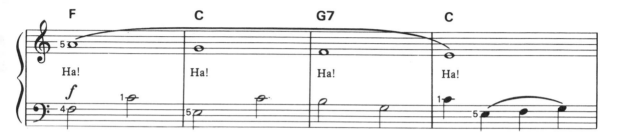

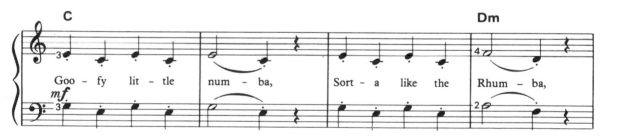

FLATS

4

A flat: ♭ against a note means play the nearest available key (black or white) to the left of that note.

The flat continues through the bar but is cancelled automatically at the next bar.

A 'natural': ♮ may also be used to cancel a flat.

The most commonly used flat is:

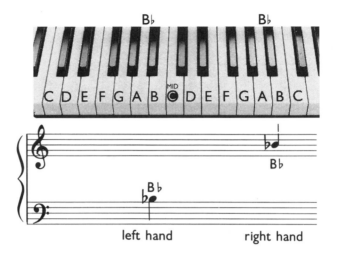

EXAMPLES OF OTHER FLATS

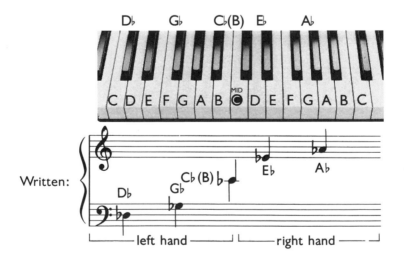

Notice that C♭ and B are exactly the same note. Sometimes it is more convenient to call B 'C♭'

LET HIM GO, LET HIM TARRY

Traditional

Watch out for 'flat' notes in this and the following piece. Remember to return to 'natural' notes.

Here the melody is taken over briefly by the left hand.

THE WINNER TAKES IT ALL

Words & Music: Benny Andersson & Bjorn Ulvaeus

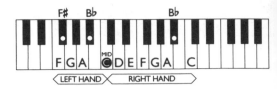

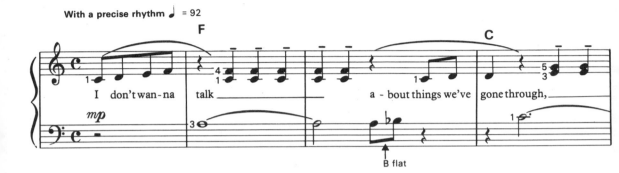

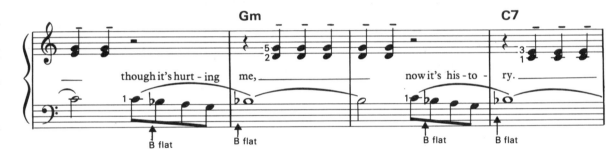

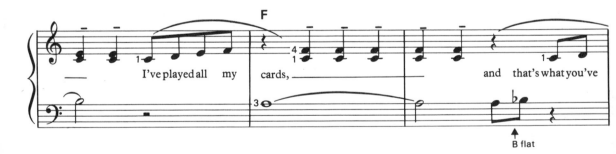

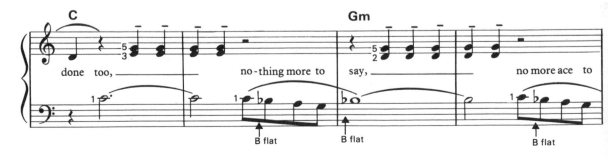

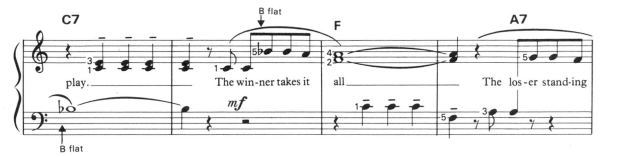

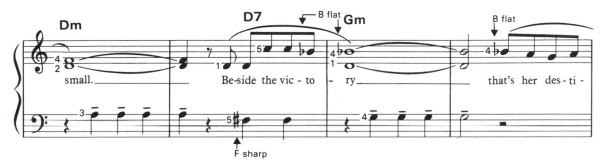

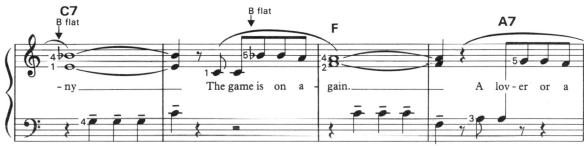

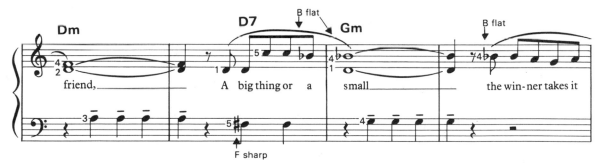

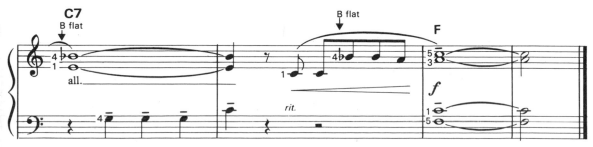

NEW NOTES

5

You are now going to learn a famous song by The Beatles. But before you tackle it, here are two new notes:

D for right hand
D for left hand

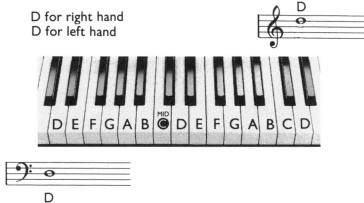

Both these notes—which are shown above—occur in your new piece, so make sure you know them.

A HARD DAY'S NIGHT

Words & Music: John Lennon and Paul McCartney

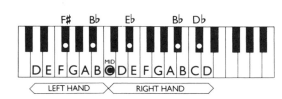

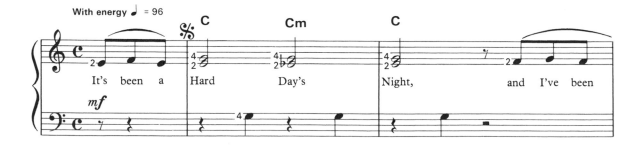

With energy ♩ = 96

It's been a   Hard   Day's   Night,   and I've been
mf

work - ing   like a   dog ____   It's been a   Hard   Day's

68

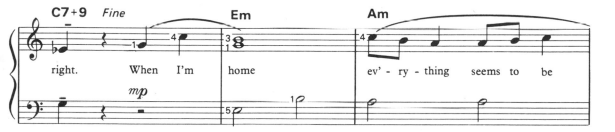

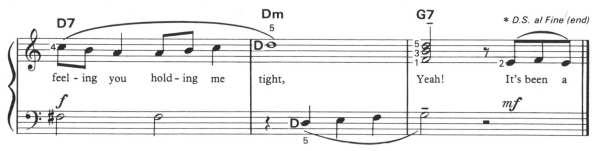

*Dal Segno al Fine. 'From the sign to the end'. Go back to the sign ℅ and continue playing until 'Fine' (the end of the piece).

SCALE OF C, KEY OF C, PASSING NOTES

6

A 'Scale' is a succession of adjoining notes ascending or descending.

The 'Scale of C (Major)' requires no black notes:

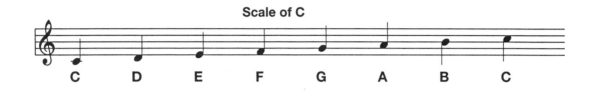

Scale of C

C   D   E   F   G   A   B   C

When the notes used in a piece of music are all taken from the Scale of C, the piece is said to be in the 'Key of C'.

PASSING NOTES

However, a piece of music in C could use notes which are not in the Scale of C. If these notes are brief they are called 'passing notes'. Passing notes are of a temporary nature only and do not affect the overall key.

In the following piece, "He'll Have To Go", look out for 'passing notes' in both hands.

HE'LL HAVE TO GO
Words & Music: Joe Allison & Audrey Allison

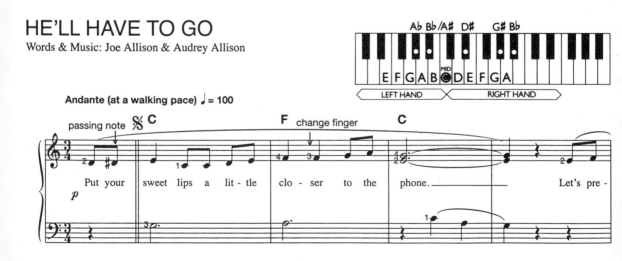

COMMON TIME AND
CUT COMMON TIME (ALLA BREVE)

The sign **C** stands for 4/4 time, that is, there are four crotchets (or quarter notes) to the bar. 4/4 is also known as 'Common Time'.

The sign **¢** stands for 2/2 time, that is, there are two minims (or half notes) to

the bar. 2/2 time is also known as 'Cut Common Time', or Alla Breve.

Pieces written in Cut Common Time have a distinct feel of two in a bar, and they tend to be faster than those written in Common Time.

THOSE LAZY, HAZY, CRAZY DAYS OF SUMMER

Words: Charles Tobias. Music: Hans Carste

72

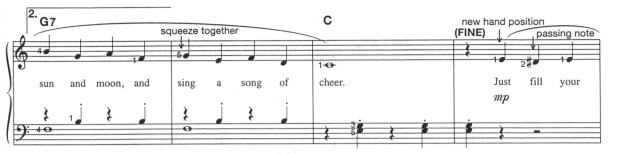

sun and moon, and sing a song of cheer. Just fill your

bas - ket full of sand - wich - es, and ween - ies. Then lock the

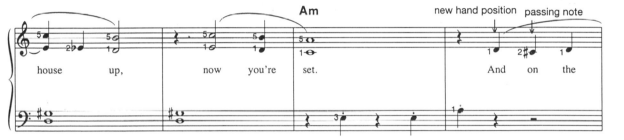

house up, now you're set. And on the

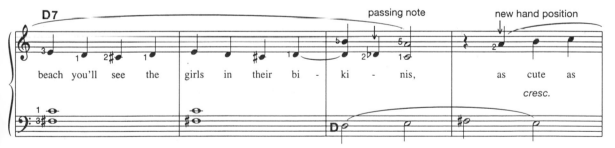

beach you'll see the girls in their bi - ki - nis, as cute as

e - ver, but they nev - er get 'em wet! Roll out those

SCALE OF F, KEY OF F, KEY SIGNATURE

8

Read lesson 6 again to refresh your memory about Scales, Keys, and Passing Notes.

The Key of F (Major) comes from the Scale of F (Major), which has one black note: B flat.

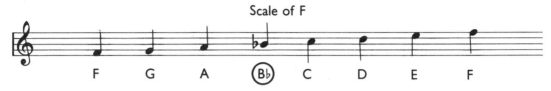

Scale of F

F   G   A   (Bb)   C   D   E   F

Pieces which are written in the Key of F (major) use the notes from the scale of the same name, although the piece may also include some passing notes.

When a piece is written in the key of F (major), it is necessary to indicate the B flats at the beginning of the piece, like this:

Key of F major

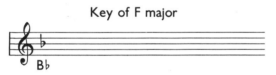

Bb

This is called the 'Key Signature'. It tells you that whenever you see the note B, you play it as B flat.

Under The Bridges Of Paris, which you are going to play now, is in the Key of F major, as you can see from the key signature.

Remember: you play all B's as B flats wherever they fall on the keyboard.

A REMINDER ABOUT NATURALS

A 'natural' sign: ♮ cancels a sharp or flat. The natural continues through the bar, but at the next bar everything reverts to normal.

UNDER THE BRIDGES OF PARIS
(SOUS LES PONTS DE PARIS)
Music: Vincent Scotto. English lyric: Dorcas Cochran.
French lyric: J. Rodor.

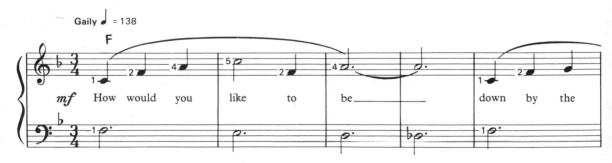

Gaily ♩ = 138

F

mf How would you like to be____ down by the

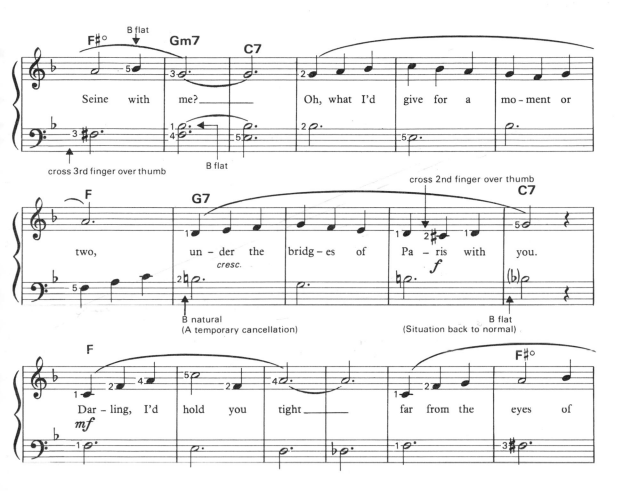

LIEBESTRÄUME

By: Franz Liszt

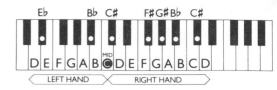

Remember: This solo is in F major.
Play all B's as B flats, unless
instructed otherwise.

change to 4th finger on A

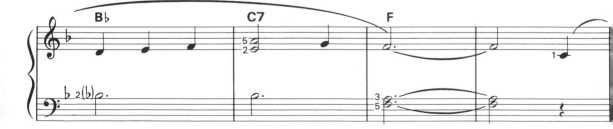

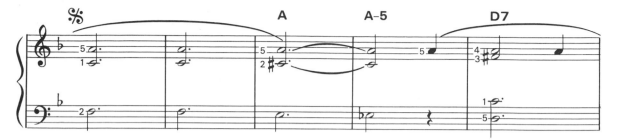

since this is a new phrase the finger may jump

Fine

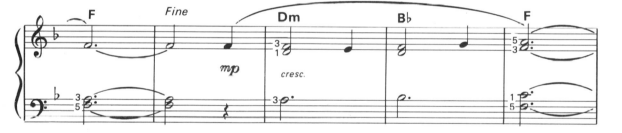

change to 3rd finger
on A

*In Time i.e. pick up the original speed

BRIGHT EYES

Words & Music: Mike Batt

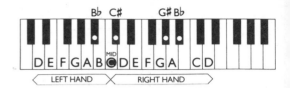

Remember: **All B's are to be played as B flats, unless instructed otherwise.**

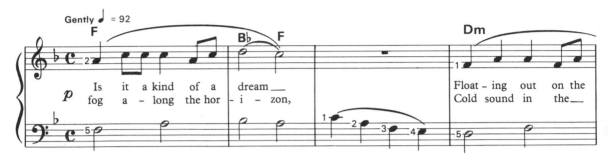

Gently ♩ = 92

Is it a kind of a dream ___
fog a - long the hor - i - zon,

Float - ing out on the
Cold sound in the ___

tide ___
air ___

Fol - low - ing the riv - er of
no - bo - dy ev - er knows

death down - stream
when you go

Oh is it a
And where do you

dream? ___

There's a

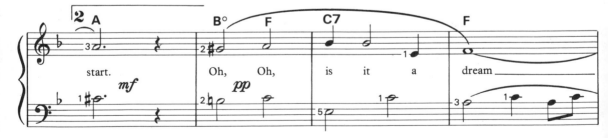

start.

Oh, Oh,

is it a

dream ___

*Repeat Marking. Since there is no matching Repeat Sign to go back to, repeat from the beginning of the piece.

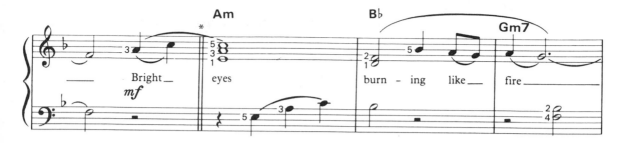

Bright _ eyes burn - ing like _ fire _____

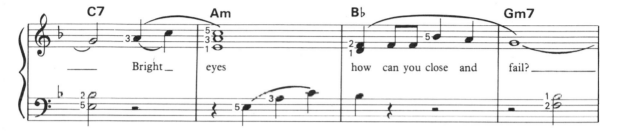

Bright _ eyes how can you close and fail? _____

How can the light that burned so bright - ly

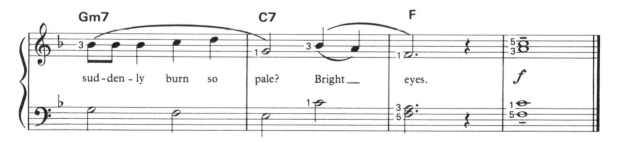

sud-den-ly burn so pale? Bright _ eyes.

*Section Lines. End of one Section of
the piece and the beginning of another.

NEW NOTES

9

Before tackling the next two pieces, here are some new notes for you to learn. Make sure that you can recognise them as soon as you see them, by practising them a few times:

E, F for right hand
C for left hand

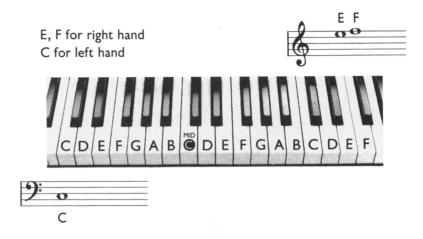

C

PLAISIR D'AMOUR
Words & Music: Giovanni Paolo Martini

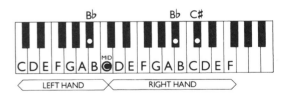

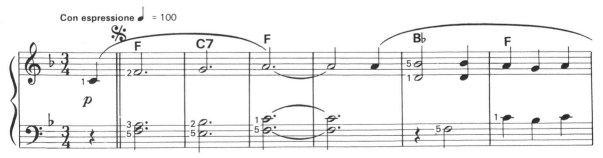

Con espressione ♩ = 100

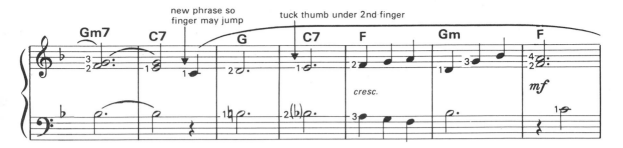

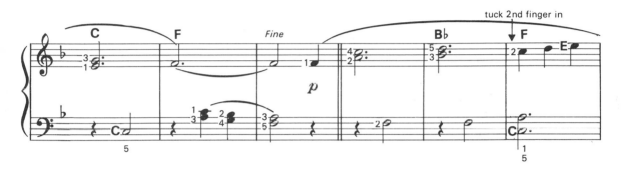

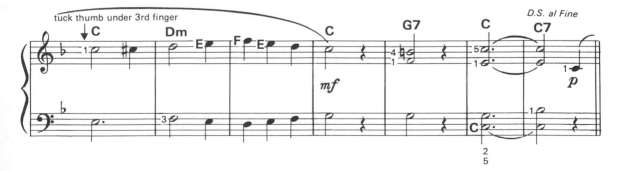

TAKE ME HOME, COUNTRY ROADS

Words & Music: Bill Danoff,
Taffy Nivert and John Denver

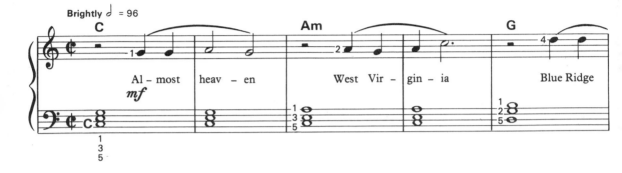

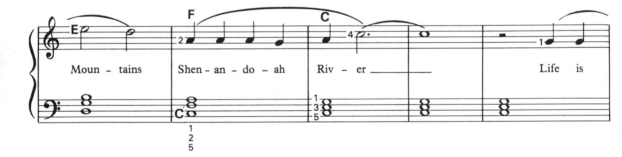

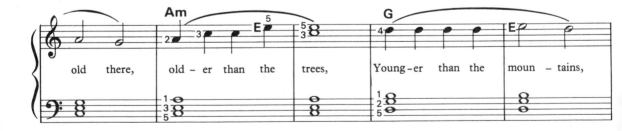

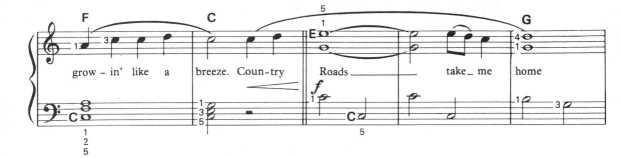

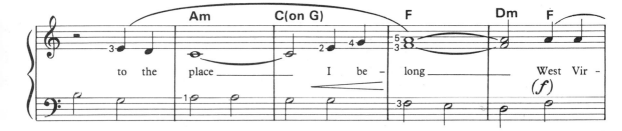

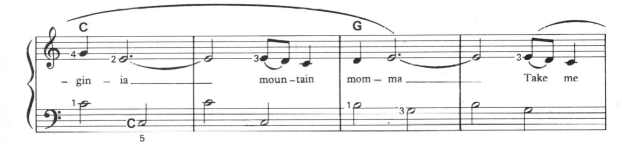

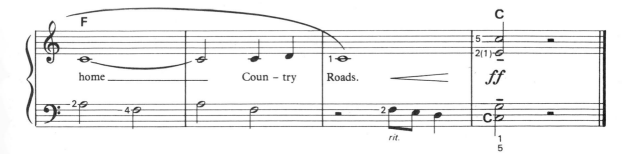

DOTTED CROTCHET
(DOTTED QUARTER NOTE)

10

A dot after a note increases its value by one half. When you apply this principle to a crotchet (quarter note) you get:

♩ crotchet (quarter note) = 1 beat

♩. dotted crotchet (dotted quarter note) = 1½ beats

A dotted crotchet (1½ beats) is almost always accompanied by a single quaver (½ beat), making two full crotchet beats in all:

♩. ♪ 1½ beats + ½ beat Total: 2 beats
or:
♪ ♩. ½ beat + 1½ beats Total: 2 beats

The first of these dotted crotchet/quaver combinations: ♩. ♪ appears frequently in the piece that follows.
It is counted like this:

SILENT NIGHT

count: 1   2 and 3   1   2   3

Pick a suitable speed for your basic crotchet beat **and be sure to maintain the same speed throughout the piece.**

BAR 1
- Play 'G' on beat 1 and let the sound continue as you count beat 2.
- Play 'A' on the 'and' between beats 2 and 3.
- Play 'G' on beat 3.

BAR 2
- Play 'E' on beat 1 and let the sound continue through beats 2 and 3.

Continue similarly through the piece.

LEFT HAND MELODY

Notice that during Bars 9-16 of *Silent Night* the Left Hand plays the melody. Increase the volume of the Left Hand at this point so that the melody can be heard clearly.

SILENT NIGHT

Words & Music: Joseph Mohr and Franz Gruber

Peacefully ♩ = 84

Si - lent night Ho - ly night All is calm,

All is bright. 'Round yon Vir - gin and ____ her child.

cross 3rd finger over thumb

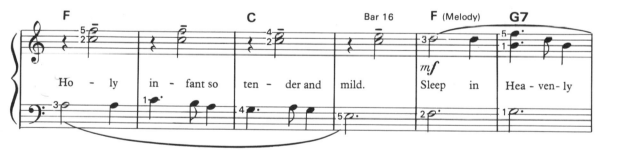

Ho - ly in - fant so ten - der and mild. Sleep in Hea - ven - ly

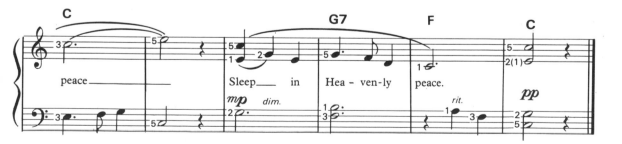

peace ____ Sleep ____ in Hea - ven - ly peace.

DOTTED CROTCHET
(DOTTED QUARTER NOTE)-2

The next song features the second of our dotted crotchet/quaver combinations.

This time the quaver is played first:

♪𝅘𝅥𝅭 ½ beat + 1½ beats Total: 2 beats

Count this figure like this:

GUANTANAMERA

BAR 1   BAR 3   (etc)

Count: 1   2 and 3 and 4   1 2 3 and 4 and 1   2 and 3 and 4

Maintain a regular crotchet (quarter note) beat throughout. It helps to tap your foot on the main beat.

BAR 1
- Play 'D' and 'F' together on beat 1.
- Play the same on beat 2.
- Play the same on the 'and' between beats 2 and 3.
- Play the same on beat 3.
- Play the same on the 'and' between beats 3 and 4.
- Let the sound continue through beat 4.

BAR 3
- Play 'C' on beat 1.
- Play 'D' on beat 2.
- Play 'A' on the 'and' between beats 2 and 3.
- Play 'C' on beat 3.
- Play 'C' on the 'and' between beats 3 and 4.
- Let the sound continue through beat 4.

Continue like this through the piece.

GUANTANAMERA
Words by: Jose Marti.
Music adaptation by: Hector Angulo and Pete Seeger.

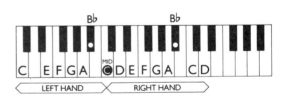

TEACHERS: * The flat has been put here for the moment because the pupil has not been taught the lower 'B' note. The normal F major key signature appears in Book 3 page 12.

cross 3rd finger over thumb
cross 2nd finger over thumb

F — B♭ — C — F — B♭ — C — FINE

Guan - ta - na - me - ra — gua - ji - ra — Guan - ta - na - me - ra! — Yo soy un

p

cross 2nd finger over thumb

Gm7 — C7 — F — Gm — C7

hom - bre sin - ce - ro — De don - de cre - ce la pal - ma — Yo soy un

Gm7 — C7 — Gm7 — C7

hom - bre sin - ce - ro — De don - de cre - - ce la pal - ma. — Yan - tes de

F — B♭ — C — F — B♭ — C — *D.C. al Fine*

mo - rir - me quie - ro, — E - char mis ver - sos del al - ma

mp

*Da Capo al Fine 'From the beginning to
the end'. Go back to the beginning of the
piece and continue playing until 'Fine'
(the end of the piece).

The next piece makes use of both the ♩. ♪ and ♪ ♩. dotted crotchet/quaver combinations.

BY THE TIME I GET TO PHOENIX

Words & Music: Jim Webb

With expression ♩ = 80

Gm7   C7   Fmaj7   cross 2nd finger over thumb   F

mf   *p*

By the time I get to Phoe-nix_____ she'll be ri - sin'   She'll

p

Count: 1 and 2 3 4 and 1 and 2 3 4 and

Gm7   C7   Fmaj7   tuck thumb under 3rd finger   F7

find the note I left hang-in'_____ on her door.   She'll

mf

B♭maj7   Gm   Am7   Dm7

laugh when she reads the part_____ that says I'm leav - in'_____ 'cause I've

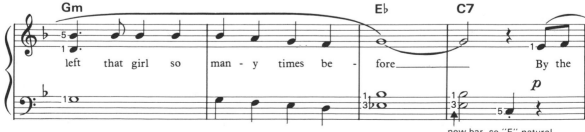

Gm   E♭   C7

left that girl so man - y times be - fore_____   By the

p

new bar, so "E" natural

WRIST STACCATO

Hand in position to strike

Down stroke

Up stroke

Learning the following piece will give you practice in wrist staccato. After each note let your hand spring up from your wrist **without moving your arm.**

Keep your wrist flexible and you will always feel comfortable when using this technique.

WILLIAM TELL OVERTURE
(THEME FROM)

By: Gioacchino Rossini

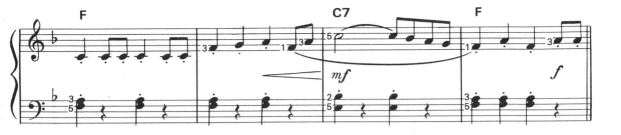

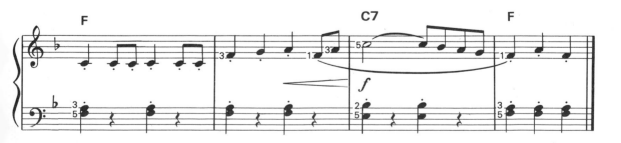

TWO TUNES WITH ONE HAND

13

Often in a piece of piano music there is a second tune accompanying the main tune. There may even be more than one secondary tune. These secondary tunes can be complete 'counter' melodies, or just short, melodic fragments put in to enhance the main melody. This is similar to choral music, where the singers are singing different tunes (or 'parts'), the whole blending together to create the 'harmony'.

On the piano, these secondary 'parts' tend to occur below, that is lower than, the main melody. Two parts are often played by one hand.

Look at bars 6 and 7 and bars 22, 23 and 24 of the following song. You will see examples of two different tunes, or parts, played by the right hand. Hold all lower notes for their full value and finger 'legato' in order to bring out the lower parts.

WHAT KIND OF FOOL AM I
Words & Music: Leslie Bricusse & Anthony Newley

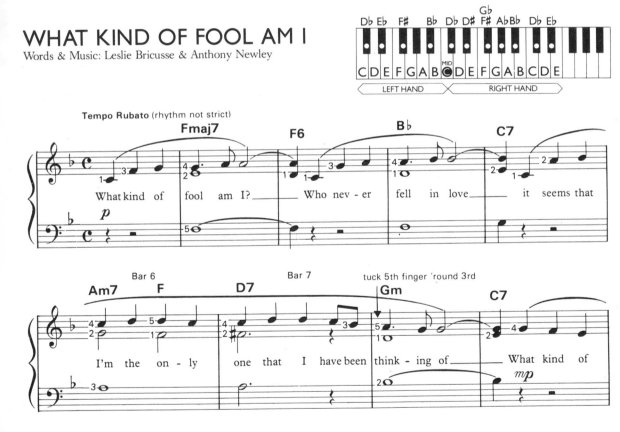

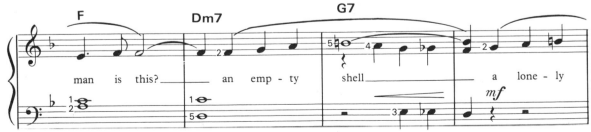

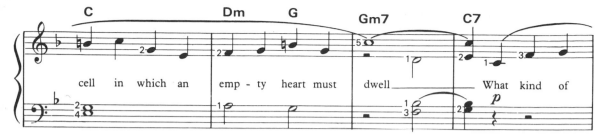

cell in which an emp-ty heart must dwell_____ What kind of

lips are these_____ that lied with ev-'ry kiss?_____ That whis-pered

slide 2nd finger from black note to white

cresc.

Bar 22   Bar 23   Bar 24

emp-ty words of love that left me a-lone like this_____ Why can't I

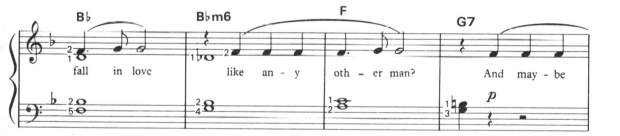

fall in love like an-y oth-er man? And may-be

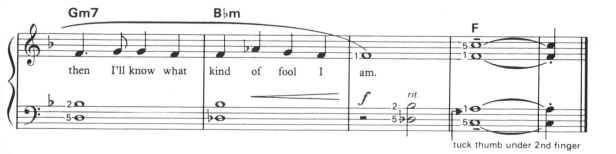

then I'll know what kind of fool I am.

rit.

tuck thumb under 2nd finger

LAST WORD

Congratulations on reaching the end of Part 2 of The Complete Piano Player!

In Part Three you will be:
- Learning new notes
- Playing in different keys
- Discovering new left hand styles and rhythms
- Developing your piano technique

Till then your last song in this Part is:

LET IT BE

Words & Music: John Lennon & Paul McCartney

Part Three

The Complete Piano *Player*

by **Kenneth Baker**

LESSONS

SONGS

CHORD PYRAMIDS

This is a simple yet effective type of accompaniment which can be used with most ballads (slow expressive tunes, often played with a rather flexible tempo).

Play the notes of the chord one by one with your left hand, holding each note down until the chord pyramid is formed. Observe the ties carefully.

SMILE

Words: John Turner & Geoffrey Parsons. Music: Charles Chaplin

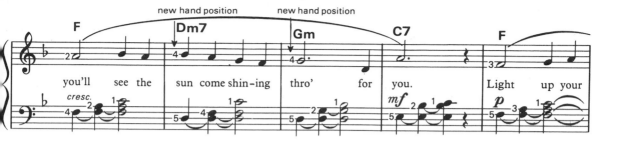

you'll see the sun come shin-ing thro' for you. Light up your

face with glad-ness, hide ev-'ry trace of sad-ness, Al-tho' a

tear may be ev-er so near, that's the time you must

keep on try-ing, Smile what's the use of cry-ing, you'll find that

life is still worth-while, if you just smile.

*Shift Technique. Sometimes necessary for good legato playing. Play F with 3rd finger then shift to 5th finger without releasing the note. The 3rd finger is now ready for use again in the next phrase.

The chord pyramid technique can often be used effectively in the right hand also, as seen in the following arrangement of *Fascination*.

FASCINATION

Music: F.D. Marchetti. English Lyric: Dick Manning

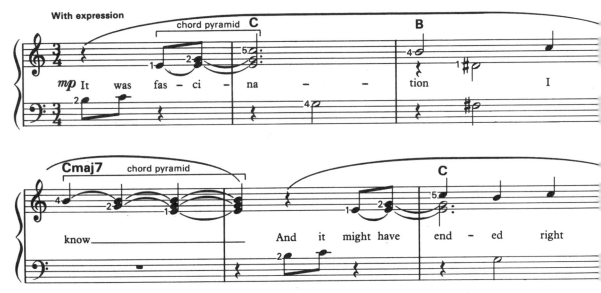

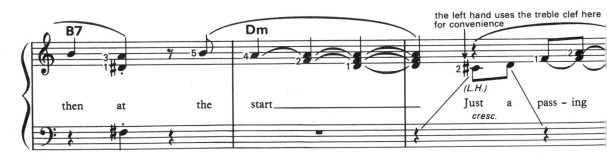

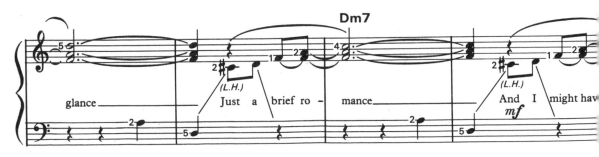

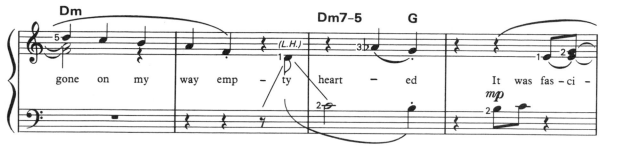

gone on my way emp — ty heart — ed It was fas — ci —

na — tion I know_____ See — ing you a —

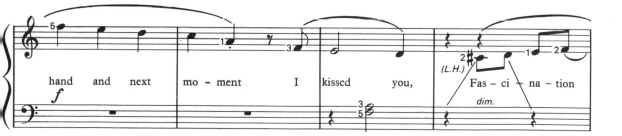

lone with the moon – light a – bove_____ Then I touched your

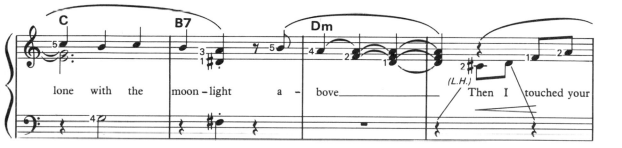

hand and next mo – ment I kissed you, Fas – ci – na – tion

turned to love._____

poco rit.

(a little ritenuto: slowing down slightly)

NEW NOTES

2

Before tackling the next song, here are some new notes for you to learn:

G, A and low B for
right hand
F, G, A and B for
left hand

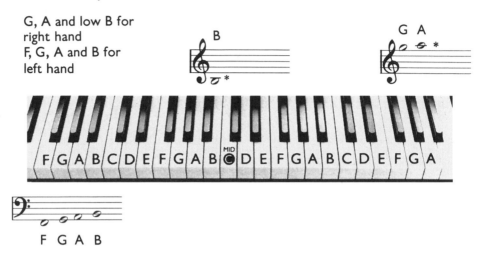

F G A B

ACCOMPANIMENT PATTERNS

Notice the repeated accompaniment patterns in the left hand in *Spanish Eyes.*

SPANISH EYES

Words: Charles Singleton & Eddie Snyder. Music: Bert Kaempfert

Ledger line: A partial line used to represent the full length line which would lie in that position (see Book One pages 15 and 16).

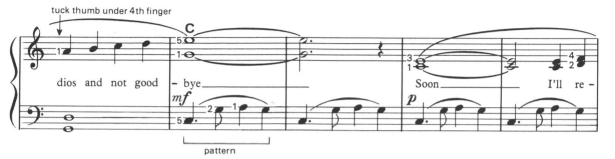

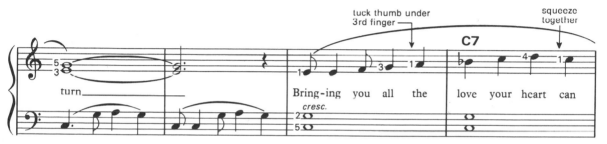

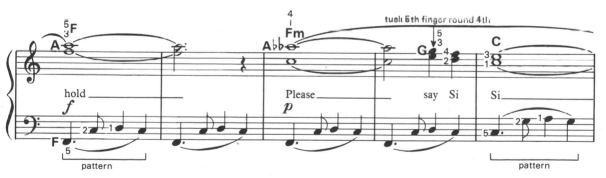

PHRASES AND PHRASING

3

A 'phrase' is a group of notes which belong together musically.
'Phrasing' refers to the way in which the notes are played.
Usually you play the notes of your phrases legato (joined up):

SMILE (Part 3, p.96)

a legato phrase

(etc.)

Sometimes you play them staccato (disconnected):

Theme from WILLIAM TELL OVERTURE (Part 2, p.90)

a staccato phrase

(etc.)

In "Dream Baby", you will be using a mixture of staccato and
legato phrasing. You will also be accenting certain notes. Such
different types of phrasing within a piece help to give it contrast,
and contrast is one of the most important aspects of phrasing.

Note the repeated accompaniment 'patterns' in the left hand of
"Dream Baby".

DREAM BABY
(HOW LONG MUST I DREAM)

Words & Music: Cindy Walker

but that won't do.____ *mp* Dream ba - by,

make me stop my dream - in', you can make my dreams come true.

mf Sweet dreams____ ba - by,____

f sweet dreams____ ba - by,____

mf how long must I dream?____

KEY OF G

4

The key of G (Major) is derived from the scale of G (Major), which requires one black note: F sharp:

Scale of G

G A B C D E (F#) G

Pieces using this scale predominantly are said to be in the key of G.
The key signature for the key of G is:

Key of G

F sharp

F sharp

When you are in this key you must remember to play every F (wherever it might fall on the keyboard) as F sharp.

BLUE MOON

Words: Lorenz Hart. Music: Richard Rodgers

sud-den-ly ap-peared be - fore me, The on-ly one my arms will ev - er

F sharp

F sharp

hold I heard some - bo-dy whis-per "please a - dore me," And when I

cresc.

looked the moon had turned to gold. Blue Moon

new hand position

F sharp

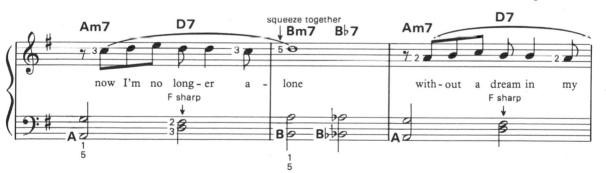

now I'm no long-er a - lone with-out a dream in my

F sharp

squeeze together

F sharp

squeeze together

heart with-out a love of my own.

new hand position

$\frac{6}{8}$ TIME

5

This means six quavers (six "eighth" notes), or their equivalent, per bar.

In $\frac{6}{8}$ time the dotted crotchet (dotted quarter note) ♩. is the basic beat, and there are two dotted crotchets per bar:

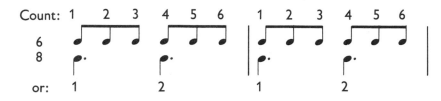

The player may count either 6 quavers or 2 dotted crotchets per bar, whichever is more convenient.

In slow pieces e.g. *Greensleeves* (p.17) it will probably be more convenient to count 6 in a bar:

GREENSLEEVES

Count: 1 2 3 4 5 6   1 2 3 4 5 6   1 2 3 4 5 6   1 2 3 4 5 6   1 2 3 4 5 6

▲
Start playing here

In faster pieces e.g. *Liberty Bell* (p.20) it will probably be better to count 2 in a bar:

LIBERTY BELL

Count: 1   2   1   2   1   2   1   2

GREENSLEEVES

Traditional

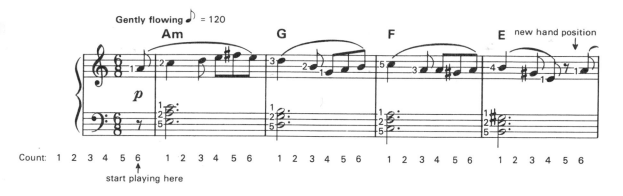

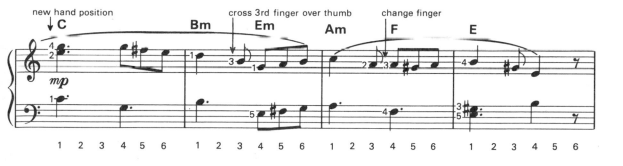

THE TWO-NOTE SLUR

6

You learnt in Part One (p.36) that a slur, sometimes called a phrase mark, is a curved line covering the notes, indicating that they are to be played legato:

and staccato).

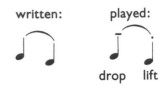

written: played:

drop   lift

play legato

When a slur covers two notes only:

stress the first note (play slightly louder); let the second note be weak (play softer

Let your hand *drop* onto the first note and *lift* up from the second note. This will give you the correct sound of the two-note slur.

I have arrowed the two-note slurs in the following piece.

NORWEGIAN WOOD
Words & Music: John Lennon and Paul McCartney

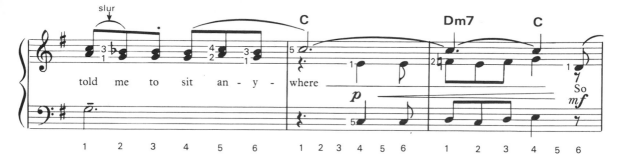

told me to sit an-y-where

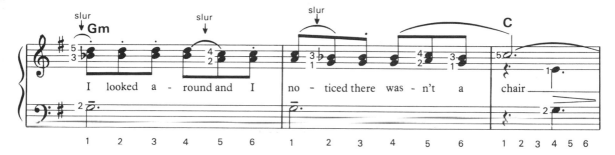

I looked a-round and I no-ticed there was-n't a chair

I sat on a rug bi-ding my

time, drink-ing her wine. We talked un-til

two and then she said: "It's time for bed".

(Pause)

NEW NOTE

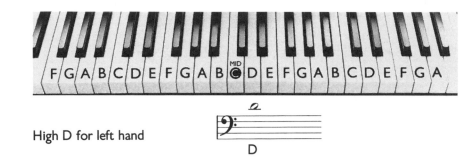

7

High D for left hand

Look for the new D note in the following
three pieces.

LIBERTY BELL
By J.P. Sousa

*A piece of music with a strongly
emphasised regular metre.

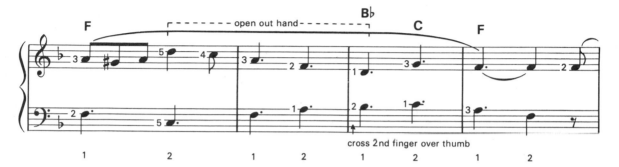

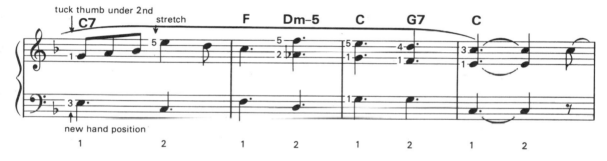

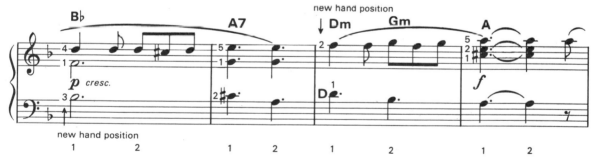

ARPEGGIO (BROKEN CHORD) STYLE FOR LEFT HAND

8

This is another useful accompaniment style, similar in effect to strumming chords on a guitar or banjo.
It is indicated by means of a wavy line:

Play the notes of the chord(s) in rapid succession upwards, rolling your wrist from left to right, yet keeping the wrist relaxed.
Sustain each note on the way up in order to get a rich, full sound.

A SUMMER PLACE

(THEME FROM) **A SUMMER PLACE**
By Max Steiner

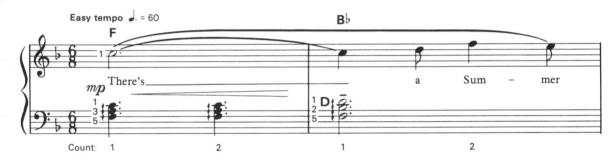

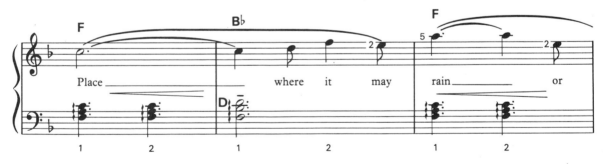

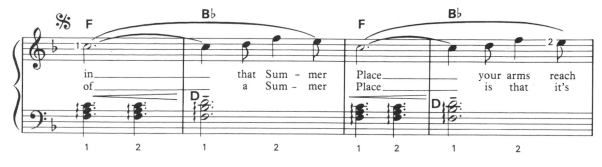

in _____ that Sum - mer Place _____ your arms reach
of _____ a Sum - mer Place _____ is that it's

out _____ to me _____ and my heart _____ is free _____ from all
an — y — where _____ when two peo — ple share _____ all their

care _____ for it knows _____ there are
mf hopes _____ all their dreams _____ all their

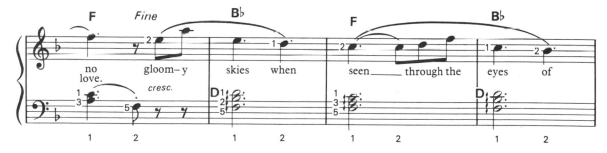

Fine
no gloom—y skies when seen _____ through the eyes of
love. *cresc.*

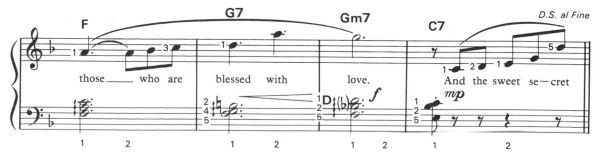

D.S. al Fine
those _____ who are blessed with love. And the sweet se—cret
mp

SEMIQUAVERS (SIXTEENTH NOTES)

9

Written:

Semiquavers move twice as fast as quavers:

Semiquavers are featured in the next piece, *Morning*, by Grieg. To get the basic timing, start by counting the piece in 6:

MORNING

Count: 1 2 3 4 5 6 1 2 3 4 5 and 6 and
(Later): 1 2 1 2

Later on you will find that the piece will flow better if you count in 2.

MORNING from 'Peer Gynt'
By Edvard Grieg

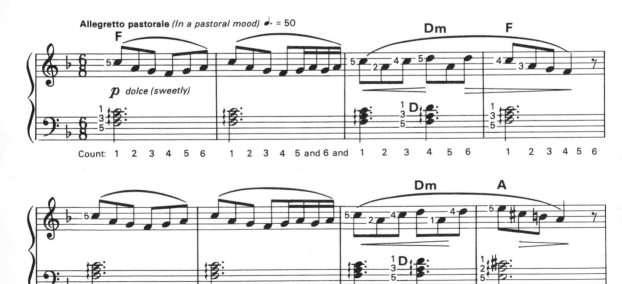

THE WALTZ

Although waltzes vary in speed, they are always written in $\frac{3}{4}$ time.

In *Somewhere My Love* (Lara's Theme, from Doctor Zhivago) observe the two-note slurs in the left hand. These will help give the piece "lift".

SOMEWHERE MY LOVE (LARA'S THEME)

Words: Paul Francis Webster. Music: Maurice Jarre

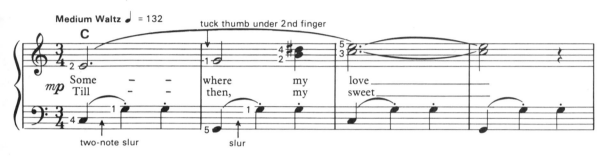

Medium Waltz ♩ = 132   tuck thumb under 2nd finger

C

mp Some — — where my love
Till — — then, my sweet

two-note slur   slur

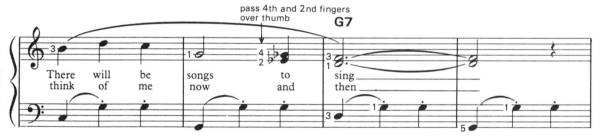

pass 4th and 2nd fingers over thumb   G7

There will be songs now to and sing then
think of me

new hand position   to Coda

Al — — though the snow
God — — speed my love

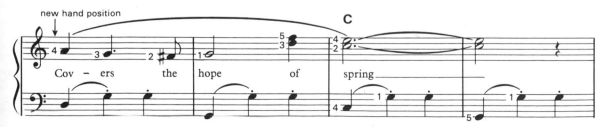

new hand position   C

Cov — ers the hope of spring

Some — — day _____ We'll meet a-

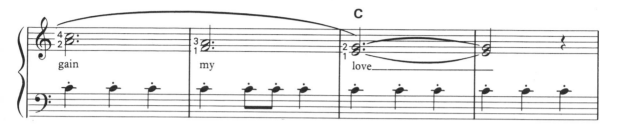

gain   my   love _____

Some — — day _____ when — ev — er the

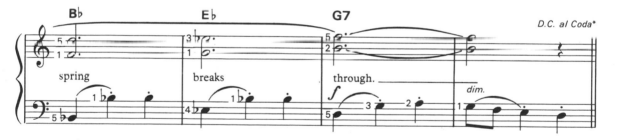

D.C. al Coda*

spring   breaks   through. _____

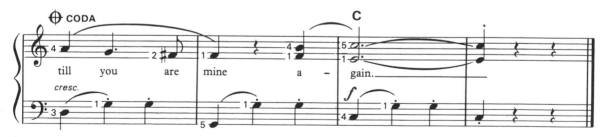

⊕ CODA

till   you   are   mine   a — gain. _____

*Da Capo Al Coda: From the beginning to Coda.
Repeat from the beginning of the piece until **to Coda** ⊕

From there jump to the **Coda** (the final section of the piece) and play through to the end.

GRACE NOTES

Grace notes are ornamental notes not included in the basic timing of the bar. They are always written small:

OB LA DI, OB LA DA

Play your grace notes as quickly as possible. So, in the above example, hold your minim C for almost its full length. Then slip in the two grace notes just before the crotchet F, which is due on beat 1 of the next bar.

OB-LA-DI, OB-LA-DA

Words & Music: John Lennon and Paul McCartney

Bright ♩ = 100

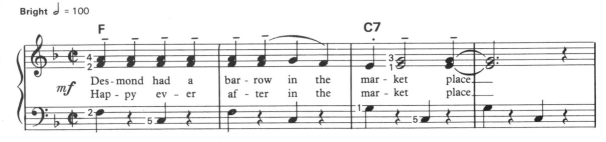

Des-mond had a bar-row in the mar-ket place.
Hap-py ev-er af-ter in the mar-ket place.

Mol-ly is the sin-ger in a band.
Des-mond lets the chil-dren lend a hand.

new hand position

Des-mond says to Mol-ly, "girl I like your face" and Mol-ly
Mol-ly stays at home and does her pret-ty face and in the

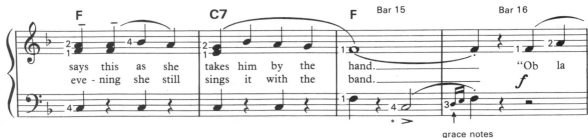

says this as she takes him by the hand.
eve-ning she still sings it with the band.
"Ob la

grace notes

*A strong accent.

118

di, ob la da, life goes on bra. La la how the

life goes on Ob la In a couple of

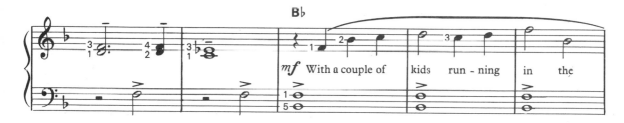

years they have built a home sweet home.

With a couple of kids run - ning in the

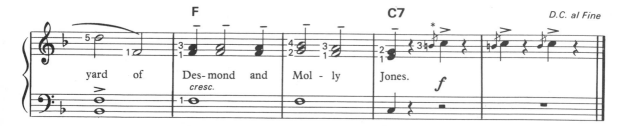

yard of Des-mond and Mol - ly Jones.

*Acciaccatura. A type of grace note. Play
the acciaccatura note as quickly as
possible.

ACCIDENTALS

12

Accidentals are sharps, flats, or naturals which are not expected, because they are not included in the key signature. In the following piece, *Over The Rainbow*, only the F sharp is expected (key of G). All other sharps and flats, and the rather frequent F naturals, are accidentals.

Remember that accidentals only apply to the bar in which they occur. At the next bar everything returns to normal.

OVER THE RAINBOW
Words: E.Y. Harburg. Music: Harold Arlen

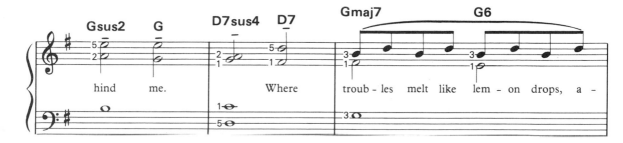

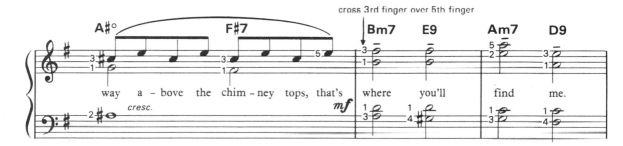

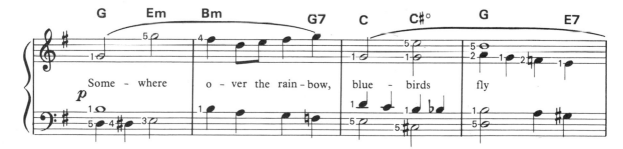

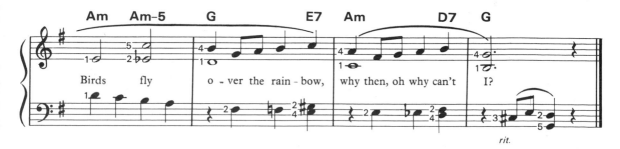

REPEATED NOTES

13 On a number of occasions in your next piece, *Irish Washerwoman*, a note has to be repeated i.e. struck rapidly twice in succession:

IRISH WASHERWOMAN

Be sure to play the first of each pair of repeated notes staccato, otherwise the note will not be ready for use again. You will find 'slur' phrasing, with the hand doing a drop-lift movement each time, a great help in these repeated note passages.

IRISH WASHERWOMAN
Traditional

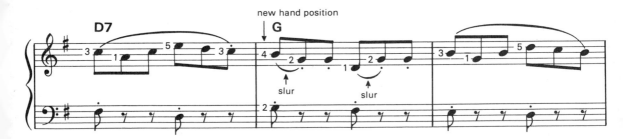

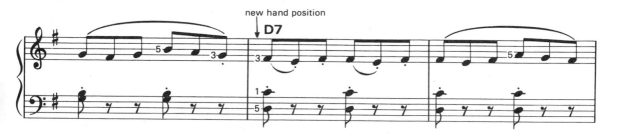

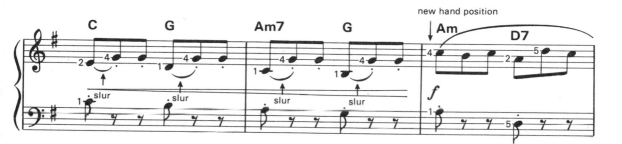

SEMIQUAVERS (SIXTEENTH NOTES) IN $\frac{4}{4}$ TIME

14

In the next piece, *Imagine*, which is written in Common Time ($\frac{4}{4}$) there are a number of semiquaver (sixteenth note) fragments mixed in with quavers, crotchets, and other time notes.

In such a situation it is probably best, at least in the early stages, to count in quavers rather than crotchets. Each semiquaver will then have a recognisable place in the count:

IMAGINE

At a later stage, when you have the feel of the timing, you could try counting 4

crotchets to the bar, rather than 8 quavers:

IMAGINE
Words & Music: John Lennon

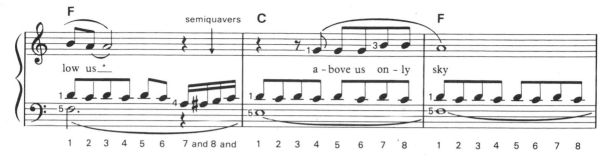

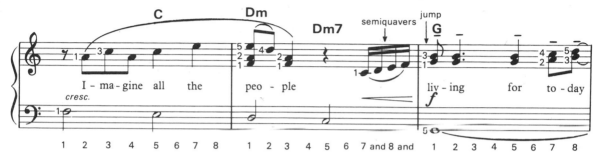

NEW NOTES

15

B, C for right hand
High E for left hand

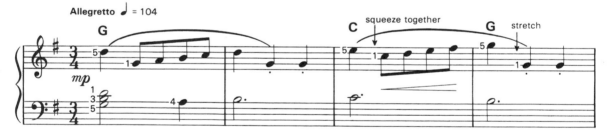

Watch out for these new notes in the next few pieces, the first of which is a charming little piano piece from the Anna Magdalena Notebooks by Bach.

MINUET IN G
By Johann Sebastian Bach

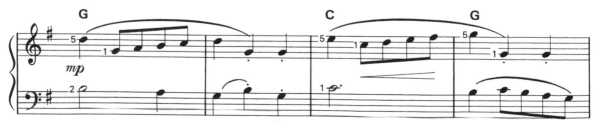

squeeze together

cross 2nd finger over thumb

new hand position

mf

new hand position

tuck thumb under 3rd finger

mp

mf

cross 3rd finger over thumb

p

E

hold for two beats each

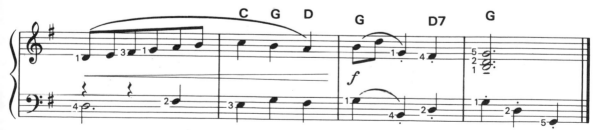

f

TRIPLETS

16

A triplet is a group of 3 notes played in the time of 2.

The most common type of triplet – the quaver triplet – is written like this:

quaver (eighth note) triplet

 or:

Compare the counting of normal quavers and triplet quavers:

normal quavers

Count: 1   2 and 3   4   and 1 2 3 4

triplet quavers

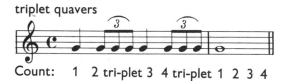

Count: 1   2 tri-plet 3 4 tri-plet 1 2 3 4

You will note that the triplet quavers move slightly faster than the normal quavers – they have to in order to fit the bar. Be sure to keep your triplet notes regular and even.

Quaver triplets appear in your next piece, *Amazing Grace*.

ARPEGGIO (BROKEN CHORD) **STYLE FOR BOTH HANDS**

In *Amazing Grace* arpeggios work their way upwards through both hands. Start with the lowest left hand note and play rapidly upwards, sustaining each note as you go.

AMAZING GRACE

Traditional

CROTCHET (QUARTER NOTE) TRIPLET

17

This is another common type of triplet. It consists of 3 crotchets (quarter notes) played in the time of 2:

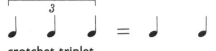

crotchet triplet

Compare the counting of normal crotchets and triplet crotchets:

normal crotchets

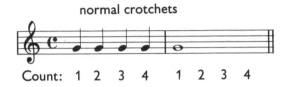

Count: 1 2 3 4   1 2 3 4

triplet crotchets

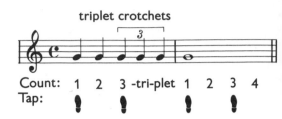

Count: 1 2 3 -tri-plet 1 2 3 4
Tap:

Tap your foot on beats 1 and 3. Start your triplet on beat 3 (a foot-tap) and be ready to play the semibreve G on beat 1 of the next bar (the next foot tap). Make sure that your triplet notes in between are regular and even.

The next piece, the theme from the film *Lawrence Of Arabia* will give you plenty of practice in both crotchet and quaver triplets.

LAWRENCE OF ARABIA
By Maurice Jarre

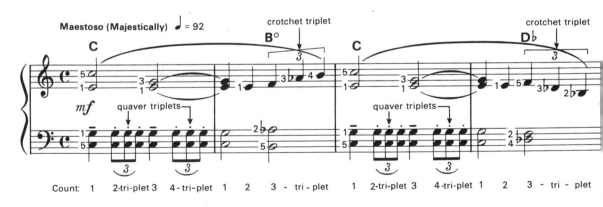

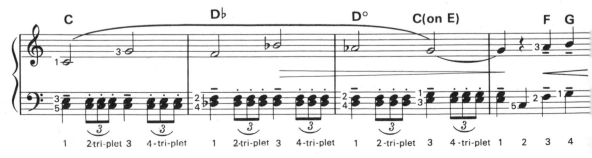

131

MORE LEFT HAND MELODY PLAYING

18

For much of the next piece, "I'm Not In Love", the melody is in the left hand part. Play your right hand chords rhythmically, but keep them well in the background so that your left hand melody can sing through.

I'M NOT IN LOVE

Words & Music: Eric Stewart & Graham Gouldman

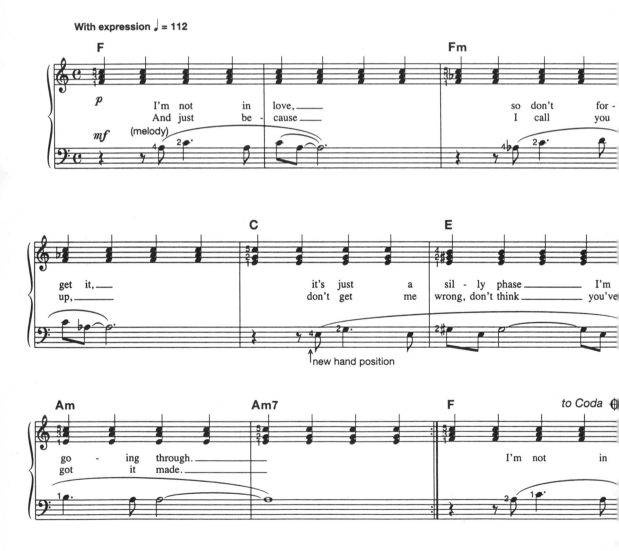

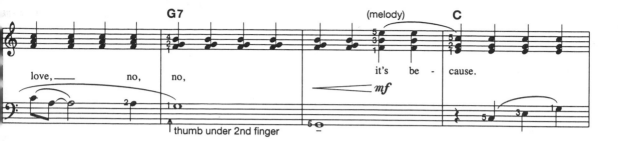

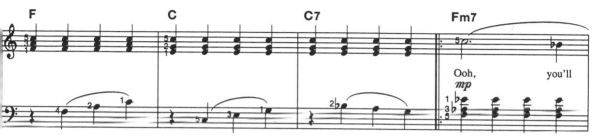

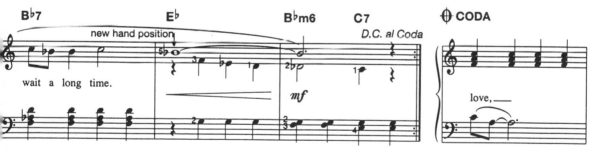

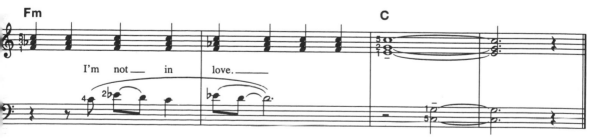

THE DOTTED QUAVER (DOTTED EIGHTH NOTE)

19

As you learnt in Part Two, (p.84), a dot after a note increases its length by one-half. So, a dotted quaver (dotted eighth note) is equal to 1½ quavers, or 3 semiquavers:

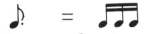

dotted quaver   3 semiquavers

A dotted quaver (dotted eighth) rest, a silence equal to one dotted quaver, is written like this:

ɤ· dotted quaver rest

A dotted quaver usually pairs up with a semiquaver, since together they make up 1 crotchet beat:

dotted quaver
+
semiquaver   crotchet

The general effect of a passage like:

is of quavers with a "lilt."

Use the phrase **humpty dumpty** as a guide to this rhythm:

say: Hump-ty Dump-ty Hump-ty Dump-ty
    ▲   ▲   ▲   ▲
   stress stress stress stress

These uneven types of rhythms are often called 'dotted rhythms'.

Look out for dotted rhythms in the next three pieces.

YELLOW SUBMARINE

Words & Music: John Lennon and Paul McCartney

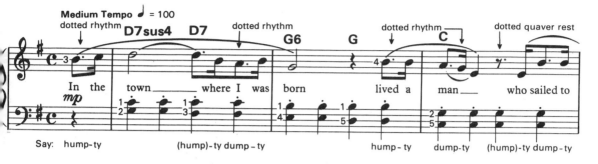

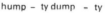

SWING

20

Swing, a jazz style developed in the 1930's, is still popular today.

One of the main characteristics of swing is its use of lilting dotted rhythms. However, in Swing a phrase like:

say: hump - ty   dump-ty

↑ stress and hold back

would not be taken literally, but played in

a more relaxed manner, like this:

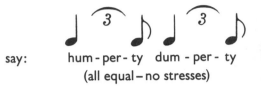

say: hum - per - ty   dum - per - ty
(all equal – no stresses)

You will be playing these sorts of dotted rhythms in *Raindrops Keep Falling On My Head*, a modern tune written in the Swing idiom.

RAINDROPS KEEP FALLING ON MY HEAD

Words: Hal David. Music: Burt Bacharach

137

LAST WORD

So we come to the end of Part Three of The Complete Piano Player.

You are now familiar with the middle range of the piano, and Part Three has introduced you to some quite advanced timings and rhythm patterns.

In Part Four you will be:
- Learning more new notes
- Adding a little syncopation
- Playing in new keys
- Using the piano pedals
- Discovering new piano techniques

Till then your last song in this Part is:

THE WONDER OF YOU
Words & Music: Baker Knight

Lyrics under the music:

When no one else can un-der-stand me When ev'-ry-thing I do is wrong.

You give me love and con-so - la - tion You give me hope to car-ry on. And you

try to show your love for me in ev' - ry-thing you do. That's the

won - der, The won-der of you.

The Complete Piano Player

by **Kenneth Baker**

FIVE NEW NOTES FOR LEFT HAND

Here are some important new notes for you to learn:

Low C, D and E
High F and F Sharp

} All for left hand

THE TOUCH OF YOUR LIPS

Words & Music: Ray Noble

Con espressione ♩ = 66

The touch of your lips
touch of your hands
up - on my brow,
up - on my head,

your lips that are cool
the love in your eyes
and
a -

cresc.

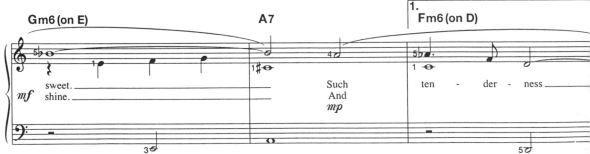

sweet.
shine.
Such
And
ten - der - ness

141

Look out for the new left hand low notes in the following piece.

TENNESSEE WALTZ

Words & Music: Redd Stewart & Pee Wee King

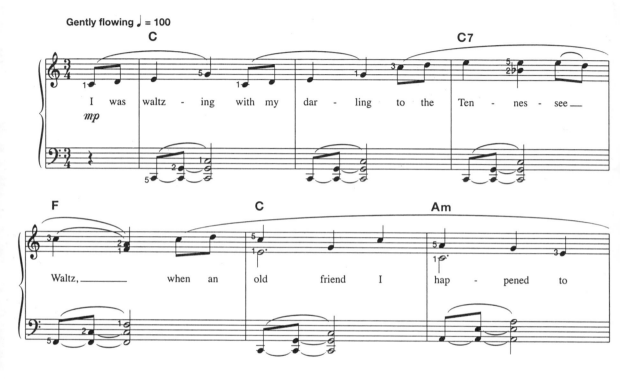

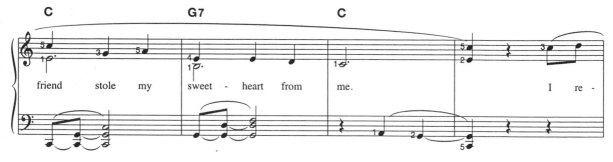

friend stole my sweet - heart from me. I re -

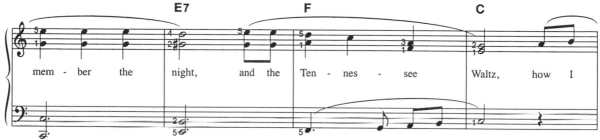

mem - ber the night, and the Ten - nes - see Waltz, how I

know just how much I have lost. _____ Yes I

cresc.   mf   mp

lost my lit - tle dar - ling, the __ night they were __ play - ing the

cresc.

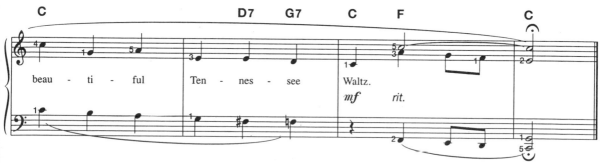

beau - ti - ful Ten - nes - see Waltz.

mf   rit.

THREE NEW NOTES FOR RIGHT HAND

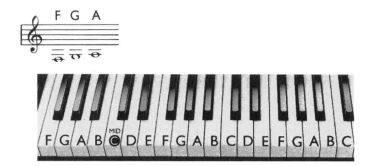

ISN'T SHE LOVELY
Words & Music: Stevie Wonder

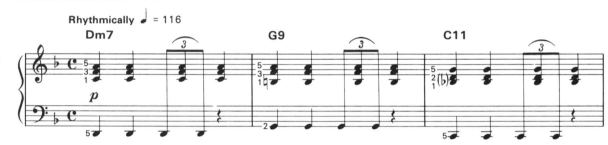

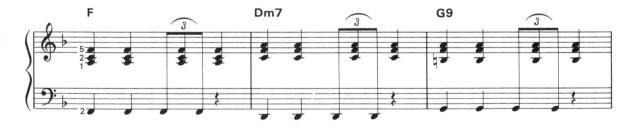

Is - n't she love - ly

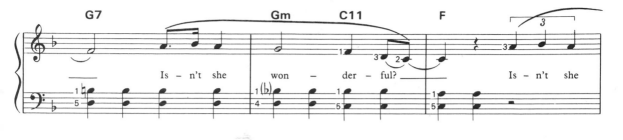

Look out for the new right hand notes in the following piece.

IF I EVER LOSE MY FAITH IN YOU

Words & Music: Sting

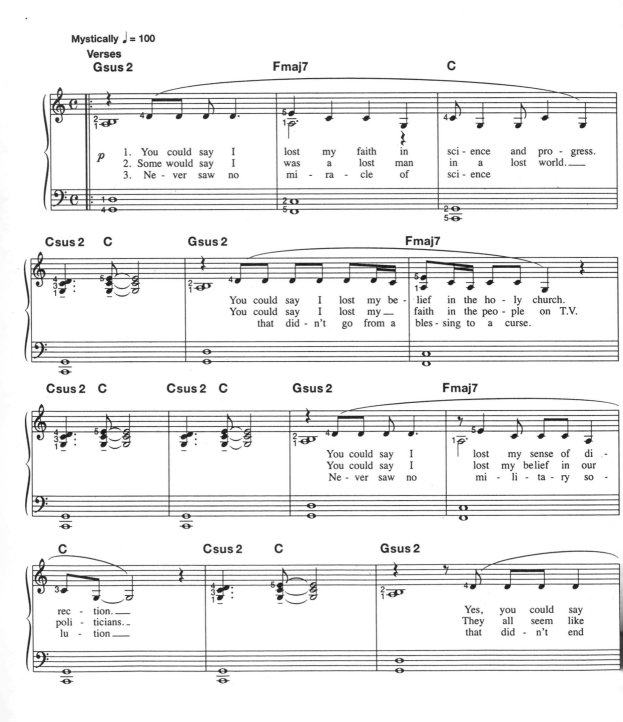

Em7 ... D (Chorus) ... E9

all of this and worse, but ... if I ev-er lose ___ my ___ faith ___ in you,
game show hosts to me, but
up as some-thing worse, but

mf

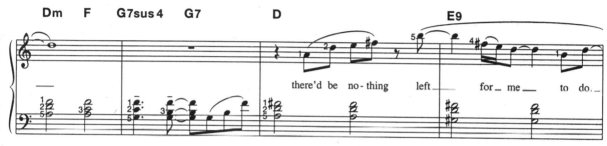

Dm F G7sus 4 G7 ... D ... E9

there'd be no-thing left ___ for ___ me ___ to do.

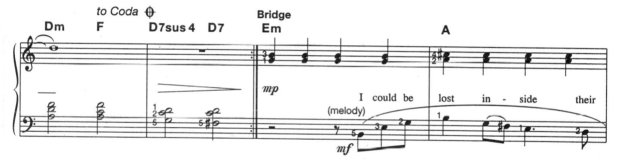

to Coda

Dm F D7sus 4 D7 ... Em (Bridge) ... A

mp

(melody) I could be lost in - side their

mf

Em7 ... A ... E ... A

lies, ___ with - out a trace. ... But ev-'ry time I ___ close my

Em7 ... Edim

D.C. (Verse 3) al Coda

eyes ___ I see your face.

CODA

G7sus 4 G7 ... A

mf

THE PEDALS ON THE PIANO

3

Soft pedal
(worked by the
left foot)

Sustaining,
or damper pedal
(worked by the
right foot)

Soft Pedal
This pedal produces a softer, lighter tone than usual. It is usually indicated in music by the words 'una corda'.

Sustaining, or damper pedal
This pedal lifts the dampers from the strings. This causes the notes played to ring on after the fingers have been lifted from the keys.

The sustaining pedal is the more important of the two pedals. There are several ways of indicating its use. The method we shall use for the moment is:

meaning: pedal down (hold pedal down) pedal up

meaning: pedal down (hold pedal down) change pedal (hold pedal down)

(i.e. lift fully then press down again immediately)

The sustaining pedal has two main functions:

1. To combine the notes of a chord:

pedal down (hold pedal down throughout) pedal up

2. To link notes in cases where it would be impossible to do so using the fingers alone:

Left hand only

(hold pedal down throughout)

Right hand only

(hold pedal down throughout)

When the harmonies of a piece change it is usual to change the sustaining pedal also:

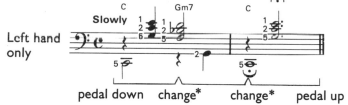

Left hand only

pedal down   change*   change*   pedal up

*(lift as new chord is played, then press down again immediately)

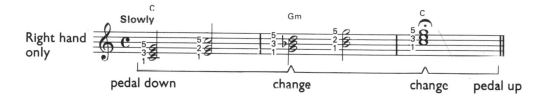

Right hand only

pedal down   change   change   pedal up

PEDAL CHANGING EXERCISE

Using **second finger only,** plus pedal, play the scale below so that it sounds completely 'legato' (joined up).

Practise this exercise until you can perform perfect pedal changes.

Here now are four pieces which will give you practice in using the sustaining pedal. Practise each piece first without the pedal. Add the pedal as you become more familiar with the notes. Observe all pedal markings carefully. When making a pedal 'change' note that as the fingers go 'down' (on the new note(s)) the pedal comes 'up'. (It will then go immediately down again).

SCARBOROUGH FAIR

Traditional

150

THE SOUND OF SILENCE

Words & Music: Paul Simon

*Although the harmony here does not require a change of pedal, the melody does.

BROKEN CHORD STYLE FOR LEFT HAND

4

In this style the left hand provides a nice flowing accompaniment by moving up and down the notes of the chord. The style is greatly enhanced by the use of the sustaining pedal, since this causes the single notes to build into full chords.

This style is different from the 'arpeggio (broken chord) style' for left hand, first used in Part Three, p.112. In that earlier style the left hand simply split the notes of the chord rapidly upwards, and involved no specific timing. Here there is a rhythm pattern present.

MY WAY

Words: Paul Anka. Music: Claude Francois & Jacques Revaux

152

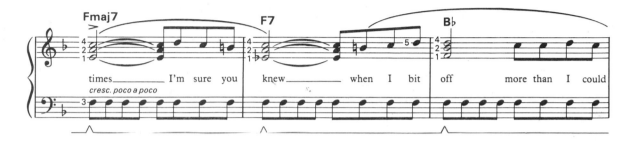

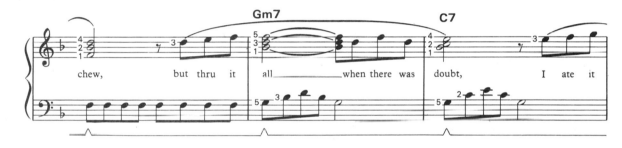

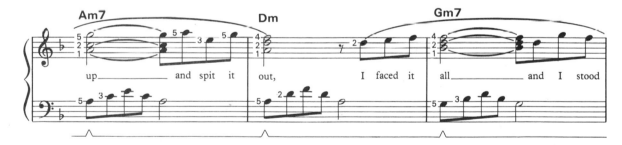

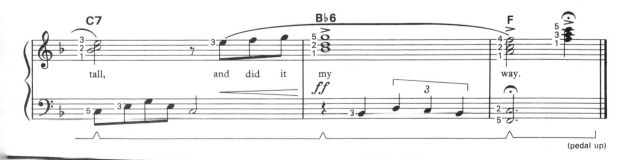

(pedal up)

Before playing the next piece turn back
to Part Three, p. 106, and read about
$\frac{6}{8}$ Time again.

(THEME FROM) VIOLIN CONCERTO (SLOW MOVEMENT)

By Felix Mendelssohn

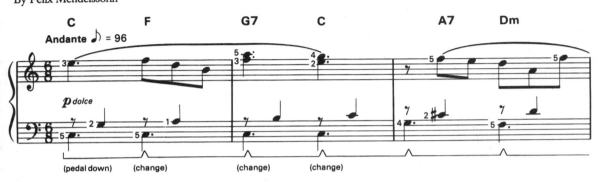

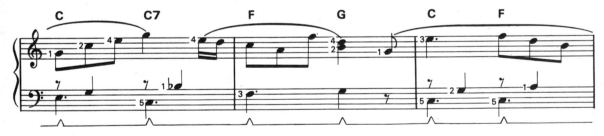

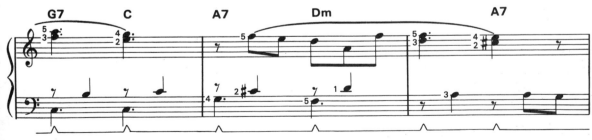

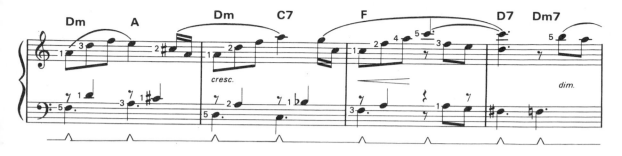

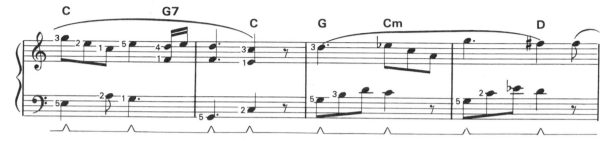

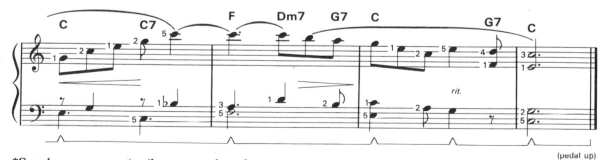

(pedal up)

*Semiquaver rest (a silence equal to the value of one semiquaver).

KEY OF B FLAT

5

The 'Key of B flat (major)' is derived from the 'Scale of B flat (major)', which requires two black notes: B flat and E flat:

Scale of B♭

Ⓑ♭ C D Ⓔ♭ F G A Ⓑ♭

Pieces using this scale predominantly are said to be in the 'key of B flat'.

The 'Key signature' for the Key of B♭ is:-

Key of B♭

B Flat, E Flat

B Flat, E Flat

When you are in this Key you must remember to play all B's and E's (wherever they might fall on the keyboard) as B flats and E flats.

THE FOOL ON THE HILL

Words & Music: John Lennon and Paul McCartney

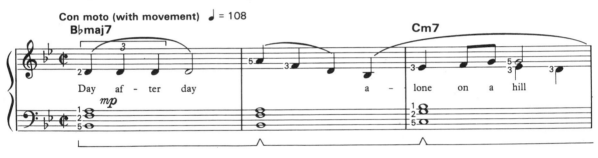

Con moto (with movement) ♩ = 108

B♭maj7 ... Cm7

Day af - ter day ... a - lone on a hill

F7 ... B♭maj7 ... B♭6

The man with the fool - ish grin is keep - ing

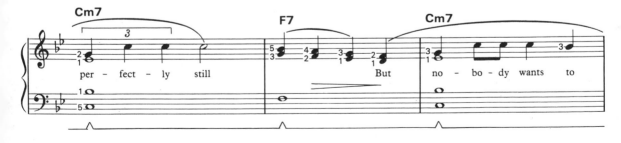

Cm7 ... F7 ... Cm7

per - fect - ly still ... But no - bo - dy wants to

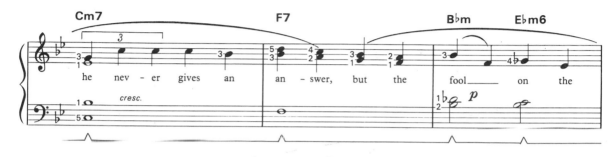

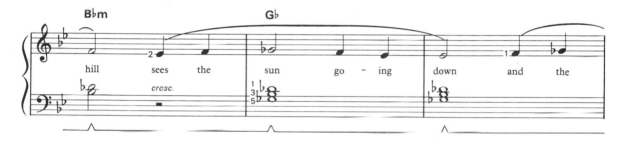

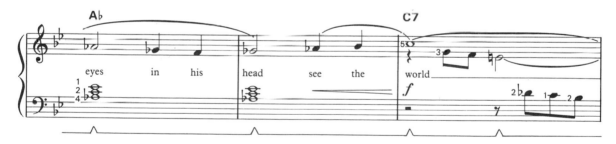

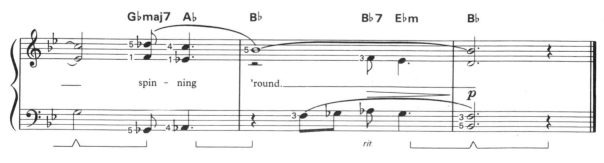

VERSE AND CHORUS

6

Mockin' Bird Hill is divided into two main sections: the 'verse' and the 'chorus'. The Verse section of a song usually contains the bulk of the narrative and is sung by a solo singer. The Chorus (the main and usually the best known section of a song) is the part where the audience joins in.

You will get a crisper effect from this piece if you do not use the sustaining pedal.

Before you play *Mockin' Bird Hill* turn back to Part Three, p.108 and re-read about 'two-note slurs'.

MOCKIN' BIRD HILL

Words & Music: Vaughn Horton

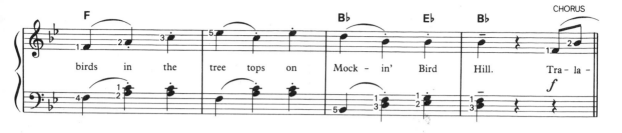

birds in the tree tops on Mock-in' Bird Hill. Tra-la-

la twit-tle-dee dee dee, it gives me a thrill to

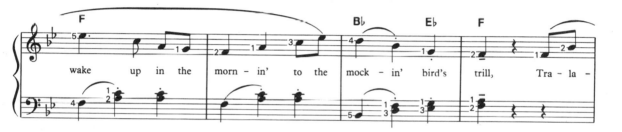

wake up in the morn-in' to the mock-in' bird's trill, Tra-la-

la twit-tle-dee dee dee, there's peace and good-will, you're

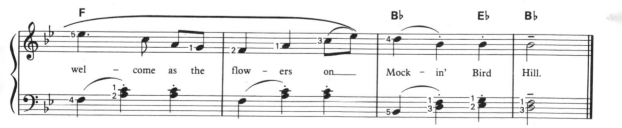

wel-come as the flow-ers on Mock-in' Bird Hill.

SYNCOPATION

7

When an important, accented note is played just before, or just after a main beat, rather than on it, the effect is called 'syncopation'.

For example:

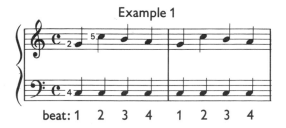

Example 1

beat: 1 2 3 4   1 2 3 4

No syncopation (each melody note is played on a main beat).

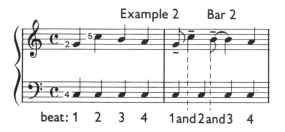

Example 2   Bar 2

beat: 1 2 3 4   1 and 2 and 3 4

Syncopation in Bar 2 (Melody notes 'C' and 'B' play **in between** main beats).

Play the second example through several times. The repeated left hand 'C's' will give you the main beats. Keep the left hand rock-steady throughout.

The above is a simplified version of the start of *Peacherine Rag*. Here now are these same two bars as you will actually play them:

Example 3 Peacherine Rag

beat: 1 2 3 4   1 and 2 and 3 and 4 and

Play Example 3 through many times to get the feel of the syncopation. Keep the left hand rock-steady and play the right hand melody notes with, and in between, the left hand notes as required.

160

PEACHERINE RAG

By Scott Joplin

Here's a famous modern piece which uses syncopation: *The Fifty-Ninth Street Bridge Song*, by Paul Simon.

Notice the Swing-style 'dotted rhythms' (see Part Three, p 136) which help give the piece a nice lilt.

I have arrowed the first seven syncopated notes for you. Try to find the others for yourself (there are eighteen more). As in *'Peacherine Rag'*, keep your left hand rock-steady throughout.

THE FIFTY-NINTH STREET BRIDGE SONG
(FEELIN' GROOVY)

Words & Music: Paul Simon

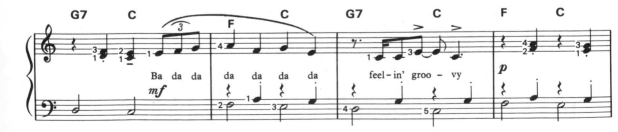

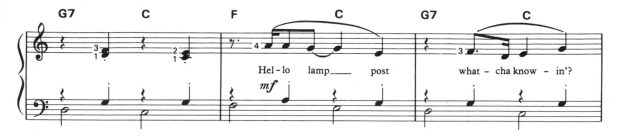

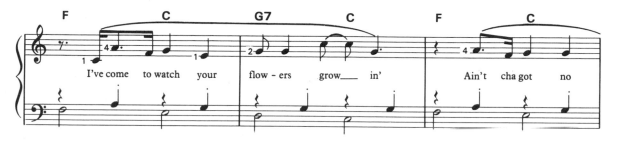

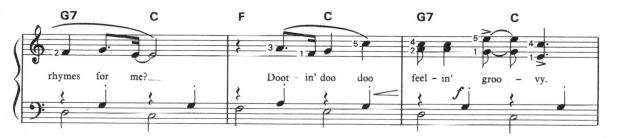

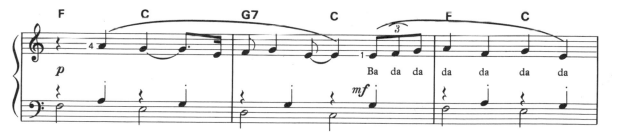

163

Latin American style tunes use
syncopation too, as can be seen in this
charming Bossa Nova* called *Little Boat*.

Since the left hand does not play on
every beat in this piece you will have to
maintain a strong rhythm in your head!

O BARQUINHO (LITTLE BOAT)

Music: Roberto Menescal. Original Words: Ronaldo Boscoli. English Lyric: Buddy Kaye

*A Latin-American dance rhythm.

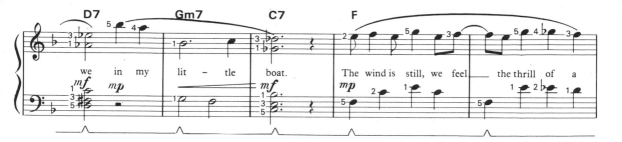

we in my lit-tle boat. The wind is still, we feel the thrill of a

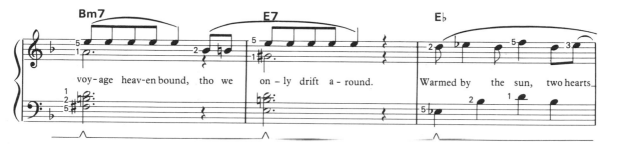

voy-age heav-en bound, tho we on-ly drift a-round. Warmed by the sun, two hearts

as one beat-ing with en-chant-ed bliss, melt-ing in each oth-er's kiss. When day – light ends and sly-

ly sends lit - tle stars to twin-kle bright-ly a-bove. It's good - bye to

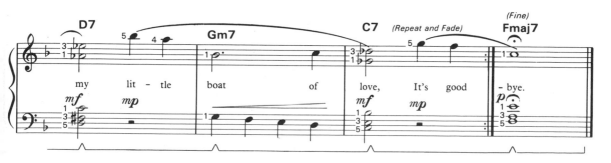

my lit - tle boat of love, It's good - bye.

In *Pushbike Song* both left and right
hands have syncopated notes (I have
arrowed the left hand ones for you).
When the left hand is not actually laying
down the beats (e.g. Bars 9-16) you will
have to maintain the time mentally (nod
your head strongly on every beat in the
early stages of practice).

THE PUSHBIKE SONG

Words & Music: Idris & Evan Jones

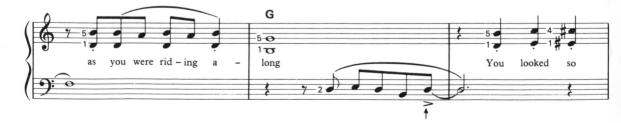

166

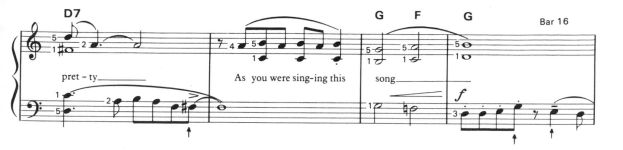

pret - ty _____ As you were sing-ing this song _____

Round, round wheels go-ing round, _____ round, round Down, up, ped - als down

_____ up, down, but I got to get a-cross to the o - ther side of town be-fore the

sun goes down. Hey, hey, hey.

*Sforzando. Strongly emphasised.

KEY OF D

8

The 'Key of D (major)' is derived from the 'Scale of D (major)', which requires two black notes: F sharp and C sharp:

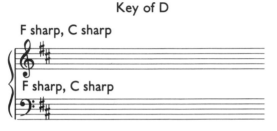

Scale of D

D E (F#) G A B (C#) D

The Key signature is therefore:

Key of D

F sharp, C sharp

F sharp, C sharp

When you are in this Key you must remember to play all F's and C's (wherever they might fall on the keyboard) as F sharps and C sharps.

Notice the Left Hand accompaniment 'patterns' in the chorus of the following piece.

DON'T CRY FOR ME ARGENTINA

Music: Andrew Lloyd Webber. Lyrics: Tim Rice

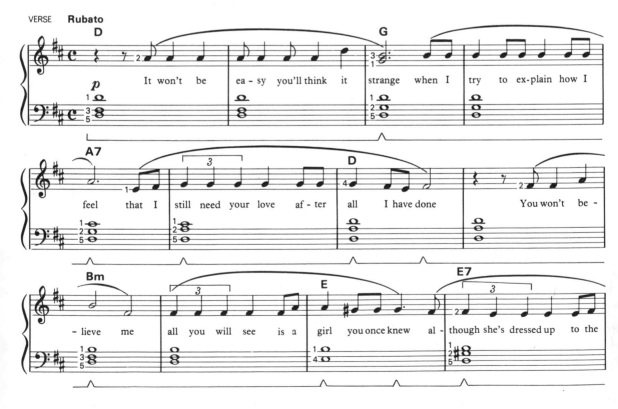

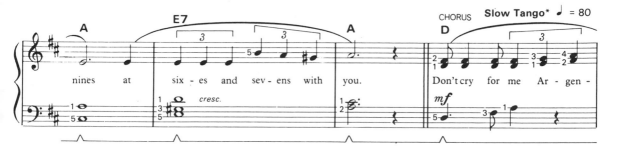

*A popular dance rhythm of African and
Latin-American origin.

169

KEY OF D MINOR

9

The Key of D Minor is derived from the Scale of D Minor, which requires one black note: B flat:

Scale of D Minor (Natural)

The key signature is therefore:

Key of D Minor

B flat

This is the same key signature as F Major:-

Key of F (Major)

B flat

Since they share the same key signature, these two keys are said to be 'related':

D Minor is the Relative Minor of F Major

F Major is the Relative Major of D Minor

Quite often in the key of D Minor you will come across a C 'sharp' or a B 'natural'. Neither of these notes appears in the scale given above. These variations occur because there are two other types of D Minor scale in common use which actually use C sharp and B natural:

Scale of D Minor (Harmonic)

Scale of D Minor (Melodic)

When in the key of D Minor remember:

1. You must play all B's (wherever they might fall on the keyboard) as B flats.

2. Look out for occasional C sharps and B naturals (they will be marked as they occur).

OCTAVES IN THE RIGHT HAND

10

This is a most important piano technique which will make your playing sound fuller and more professional.

First practise playing a scale (the scale of C will do) with your right hand to get the feeling of 'octaves' (a distance of eight notes):

Scale of C

(Repeat ad lib)

Try other scales similarly.

Next go over some of the easier pieces in the previous Parts, playing your right hand in octaves throughout.

Note: if the size of your hand allows, finger all black note octaves: $\frac{4}{1}$ rather than: $\frac{5}{1}$. This makes for smoother playing.

The next piece: *'The Green Leaves Of Summer'* is in the key of D Minor.

In the first part your left hand will be using a technique which you have seen before: 'chord pyramids' (see Part Three, p.96).

In the second part your right hand will play the melody in 'octaves'. Since this involves jumping about you will need to use the sustaining pedal to make this section sound 'legato'.

THE GREEN LEAVES OF SUMMER

Words: Paul Francis Webster. Music: Dimitri Tiomkin

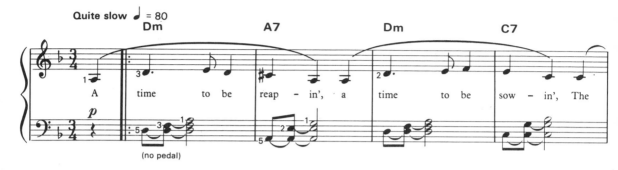

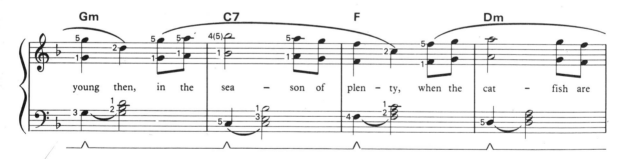

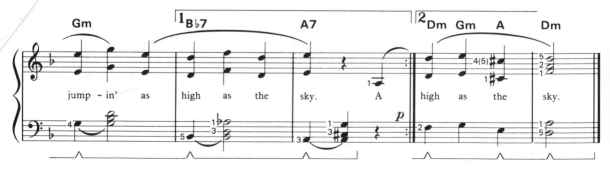

'Hava Nagila' (in the key of D minor) will give you further practice in right hand octaves.

If you have a large hand, finger the 'black note' octaves ⁴₁: if not you will have to finger all octaves ⁵₁.

HAVA NAGILA

Traditional

KEY OF E MINOR

E Minor is the 'Relative Minor' of G Major,
both keys requiring one sharp: F sharp:

The 'accidentals'* likely to occur in the key of
E Minor (due to other forms of the E Minor
Scale) are: **D♯ and C♯**

A TASTE OF HONEY

Words: Ric Marlow. Music: Bobby Scott

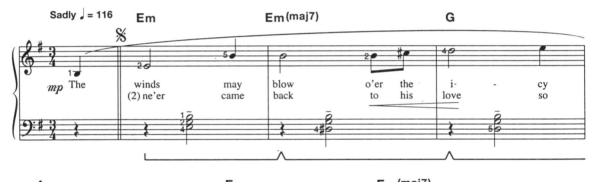

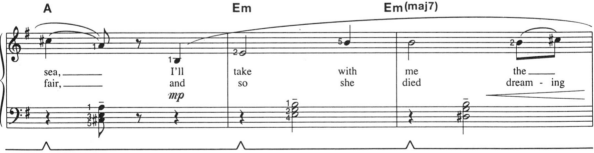

*temporary sharps, flats, or naturals.

174

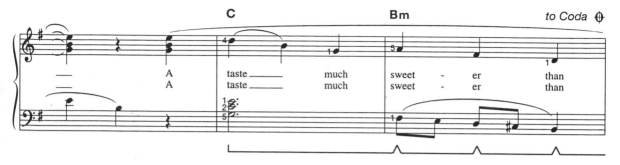

C   Bm   *to Coda* ⊕

A taste _____ much sweet - er than
A taste _____ much sweet - er than

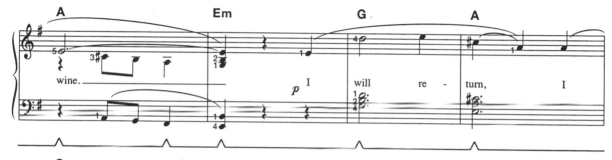

A   Em   G   A

wine.   *p* I will re - turn, I

G   A   C   Bm

will re - turn. I'll come back for my ho - ney and
mf

⊕ **CODA**

Em   A   Em   *D.S. al Coda*   A   Em

you. _____   2. He   wine. _____   A
    mp   *p*

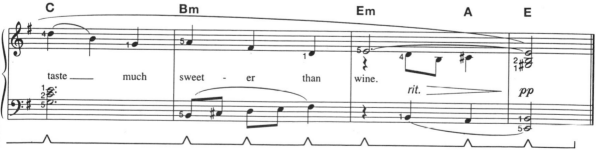

C   Bm   Em   A   E

taste _____ much sweet - er than wine.
rit.   *pp*

ALTERNATIVE PEDAL MARKING

12

An alternative and simpler method of indicating the sustaining pedal will be used from now on:

P means 'apply' or 'change' the pedal, the equivalent of: ⌐_____ or: _____⌃
* means 'lift' the Pedal.

LEFT HAND FILLS

13

In *Laura* your left hand will be playing 'fills' or 'fill-ins'. These are short melodic fragments which fill in the 'dead spots' in the right hand part and help keep the piece moving. Play all your fills 'legato' and with expression.

LAURA
Words: Johnny Mercer. Music: David Raksin

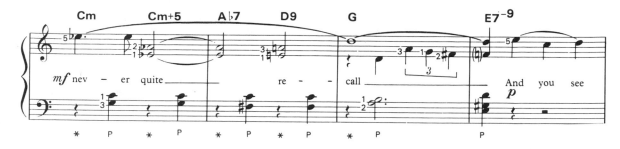

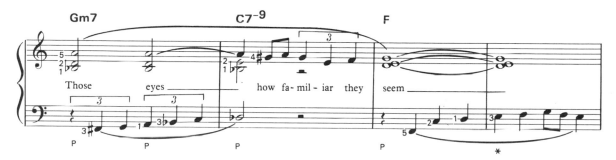

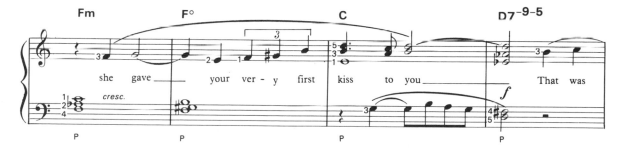

BOSSA NOVA RHYTHM PATTERN

14

In the next piece you play a simple, but effective Bossa Nova rhythm pattern in your left hand:

The pattern begins in Bar 5 and continues through most of the first part of the song.

count: 1   2 and 3   4

JUST THE WAY YOU ARE

Words & Music: Billy Joel

Wistfully ♩ = 116

mp

Don't go chang - ing____ To try and please me____
Would not leave you____ In time of trou - ble____

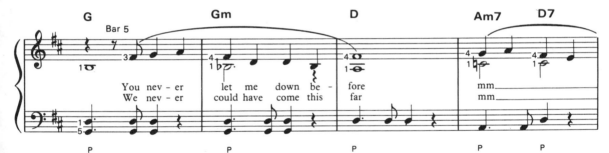

You nev - er let me down be - fore
We nev - er could have come this far

mm____
mm____

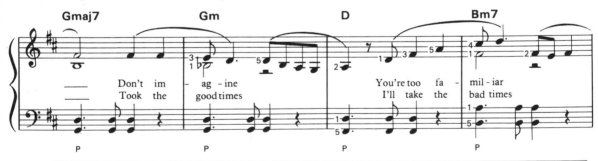

Don't im - ag - ine good times You're too fa - mil - iar
Took the good times I'll take the bad times

And I don't see you an - y more____

mf

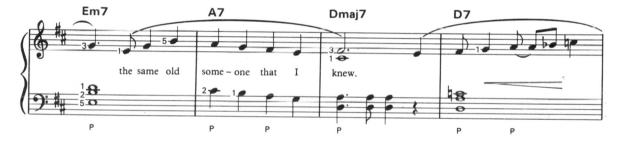

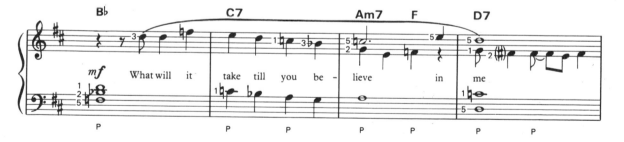

KEY OF G MINOR

15

G Minor is the 'Relative Minor' of B flat Major, both keys requiring two flats: B flat and E flat:

Scale/Key of B♭ (Major)

Scale/Key of G Minor

The accidentals likely to occur in the Key of G Minor are: F♯ and E♮

The following piece begins in the key of G Minor and modulates (i.e. changes key) in the last section to B♭ Major.

(THEME FROM) SYMPHONY NO. 40

By W.A. Mozart

Allegro moderato (Moderately fast) ♩ = 92

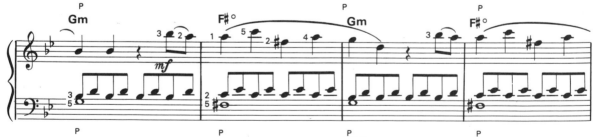

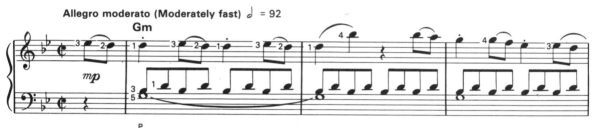

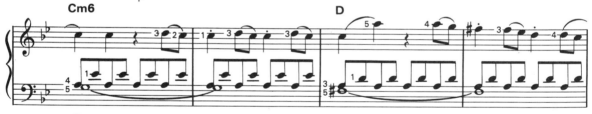

180

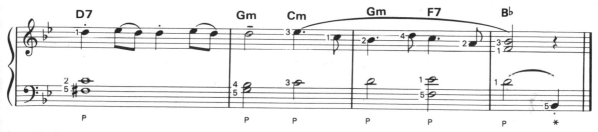

LAST WORD

Congratulations on reaching the end of Part Four of 'The Complete Piano Player'.

In Part Five You will be:
- Playing in $\frac{12}{8}$ time
- Playing in more new keys
- Adding left hand octaves
- Improving your phrasing
- Learning exciting new modern styles.

Till then your last song in this Part is:

THANK YOU FOR THE MUSIC

Words & Music: Benny Andersson & Bjorn Ulvaeus

The Complete Piano Player

by **Kenneth Baker**

WRIST STACCATO AGAIN

We begin Part Five with a lively little number called *Birdie Song*.

The Chorus of this piece is a further exercise in 'wrist staccato' for the right hand (look again at Part Two, page 90). Let the hand 'bounce' freely from the wrist joint.

BIRDIE SONG/BIRDIE DANCE

Words & Music: Werner Thomas & Terry Rendall

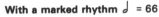

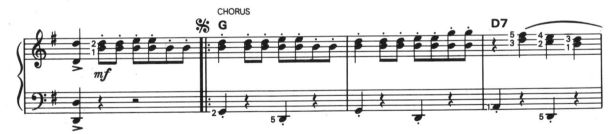

INTERLUDE

PLAYING IN ¹²⁄₈ TIME

2

When a piece of music has a time signature of ¹²⁄₈ it means that there are twelve quavers, or their equivalent, per bar.

As in ⁶⁄₈ Time (see Part Three, page 106). the quavers are grouped into 'threes':

Example 1

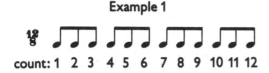

count: 1 2 3 4 5 6 7 8 9 10 11 12

A more typical ¹²⁄₈ bar might look like this:

Example 2

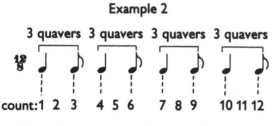

count:1 2 3 4 5 6 7 8 9 10 11 12

Although it is sometimes desirable to count the full twelve quavers in a bar (for instance, in the early stages of practice, when you are playing the piece very slowly), it is usually simpler to count four dotted crotchets (dotted quarter notes) in a bar:

Example 1

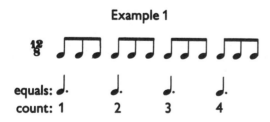

equals: ♩. ♩. ♩. ♩.
count: 1 2 3 4

Any subdivisions of the beat that occur can be counted as 'a-and':

Example 1

count: 1 - a-and 2- a-and 3 - a -and 4- a-and

Example 2

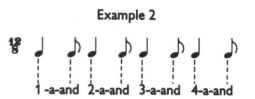

1 -a-and 2-a-and 3-a-and 4-a-and

In Example 1 you play on every beat and every subdivision of the beat; in Example 2 you play on every beat and every 'and' part of the beat. **Remember:** your '1-a-and, 2-a-ands', etc. must be perfectly regular and even, like the ticking of a clock.

With practice you should be able to drop the 'a-and' subdivisions and count only the main beats: '1, 2, 3, 4...'

Your first piece in $\frac{12}{8}$ Time is a traditional American song which has reappeared over the years in various modern arrangements. It's called: *The House Of The Rising Sun*. Here are various ways of 'counting' the melody (which way you choose depends on your stage of practice, and your familiarity with the tune):

THE HOUSE OF THE RISING SUN (Bars 1-4)

Your second piece in $\frac{12}{8}$ Time is *What A Wonderful World* (page 12). This features a typical modern $\frac{12}{8}$ rhythm pattern in the left hand:

count: 1 car-a-van 2 - a-and 3 car-a-van 4 - a-and

Say 'one caravan...' as in normal speech, but be sure to play **only on the syllables shown above.** This should give you the correct sound of this rhythm. Notice that the complete rhythm pattern consists of a 'caravan' group, followed by a simple '2-a-and' group, followed by another 'caravan' group, followed by a simple '4-a-and' group, and so on.

HOUSE OF THE RISING SUN

Traditional

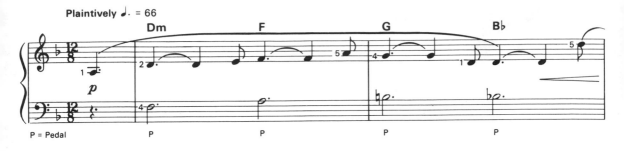

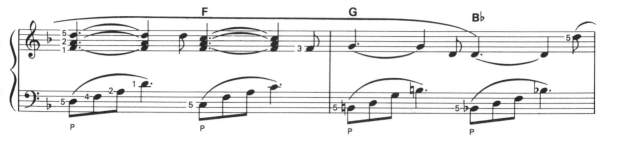

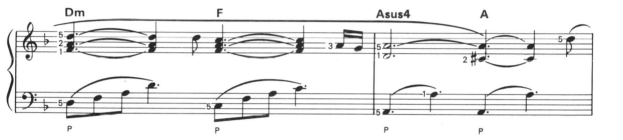

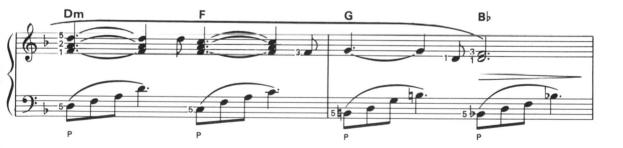

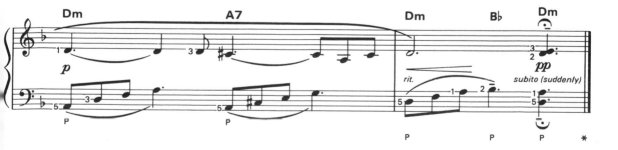

WRIST STACCATO FOR LEFT HAND

3

In the following piece: *What A Wonderful World*, you will be using 'wrist staccato' in your left hand.
Look again at Part Two, page 90. Everything said there about wrist staccato for right hand can be applied equally well to your left hand. Above all don't let your wrist become too tight; let the hand 'bounce' freely from the wrist joint.

Before you play *What A Wonderful World*, turn back to page 187 and read again about the counting of the left hand rhythm patterns in this piece.

WHAT A WONDERFUL WORLD
Words & Music: George David Weiss & Bob Thiele

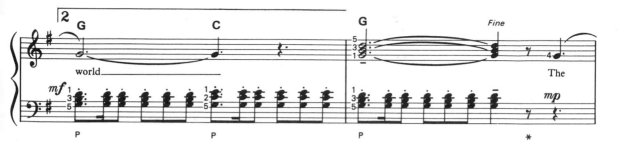

2

G   C   G   *Fine*

world_____ The

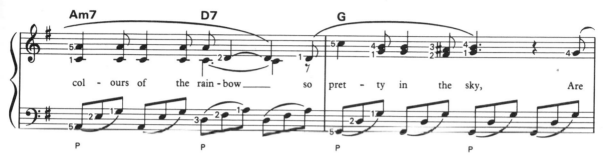

Am7   D7   G

col - ours of the rain - bow___ so pret - ty in the sky, Are

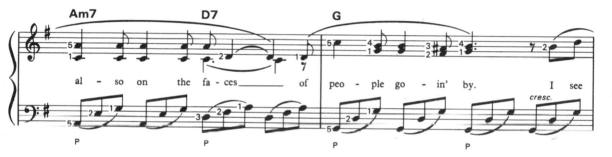

Am7   D7   G

al - so on the fa - ces___ of peo - ple goin' by. I see

Em   Bm   Em   Bm

friends shak - in' hands say - in' "How do you do!"

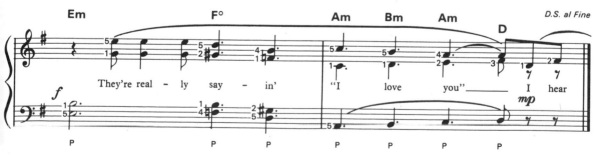

Em   F°   Am   Bm   Am   *D.S. al Fine*

They're real - ly say - in' "I love you"___ I hear

LEFT HAND OCTAVES

4

In the next two pieces: *Swingin' Shepherd Blues*, and *Yesterday*, you will be playing octaves in your left hand. In *Swingin' Shepherd Blues*, for the sake of simplicity, finger all these octaves (including those on black notes) $\frac{1}{5}$.

Before you start to play, practise the scale of C (and any other scales) in left hand octaves, just to get the feel of the distance (see Part Four, page 171 - Right Hand Octaves).

In *Swingin' Shepherd Blues* pay particular attention to the 'phrasing' (staccato, accent, and phrase marks). This piece is another good example of 'syncopation' (see Part Four, page 160).

SWINGIN' SHEPHERD BLUES
Words: Rhoda Roberts and Kenny Jacobson. Music: Moe Koffman

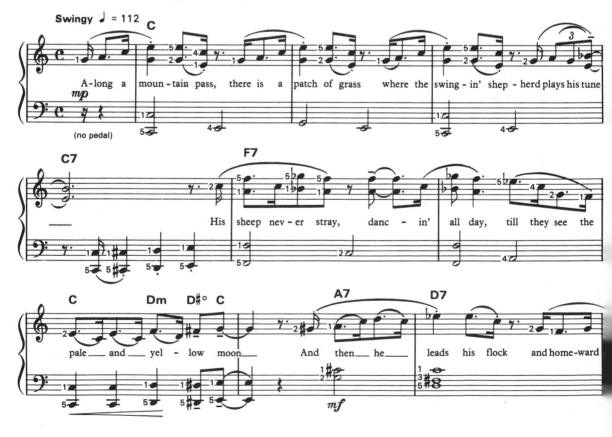

they all rock to___ the tune of The Swing-in' Shep-herd Blues. *mp*

KEY OF E FLAT

5

The Key of E Flat (major) is derived from the Scale of E Flat (major), which requires three black notes: B Flat, E Flat, and A Flat:

Scale of E♭

(E♭) F G (A♭) (B♭) C D (E♭)

Pieces using this scale predominantly are said to be in the 'Key of E Flat'.

The 'Key Signature' for the Key of E♭ is:

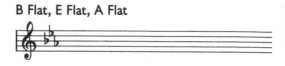

Key of E♭

B Flat, E Flat, A Flat

When you are in this Key you must remember to play all B's, E's, and A's (wherever they might fall on the keyboard) as B Flats, E Flats, and A Flats.

In *Yesterday* you will be playing left hand octaves more or less throughout. On the white note octaves use fingering $\frac{1}{5}$. On the black note octaves use fingering $\frac{1}{4}$ if this comes easily to you, if not, use $\frac{1}{5}$.

YESTERDAY

Words & Music: John Lennon and Paul McCartney

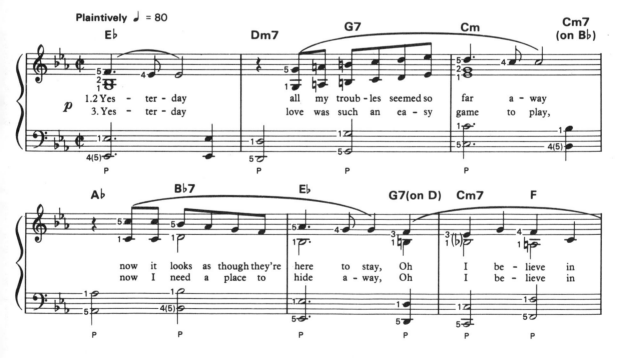

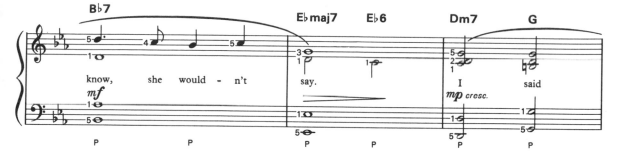

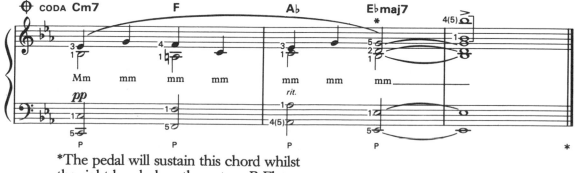

*The pedal will sustain this chord whilst
the right hand plays the octave B Flat.

DYNAMICS IN MUSIC

6

Dynamics in music are the 'louds', 'softs', 'crescendos', and the like, which help give the music life.

Your next piece: *Together*, depends for its effect on interesting dynamics. Make the most of the little 'echoes' of the tune (Bars 4, 8, 12, etc.). Play the main parts of the melody

here '*mf*', followed by the echoes '*pp*'. Build to a strong climax in Bars 27 and 28, then taper off to nothing during the last line of the piece, and include a long 'rallentando' (gradual slowing down).

Notice the way the left hand part 'borrows' the Treble Clef for those rather high notes in the 'echoes' bars.

TOGETHER
Words & Music: B.G. De Sylva, Lew Brown & Ray Henderson

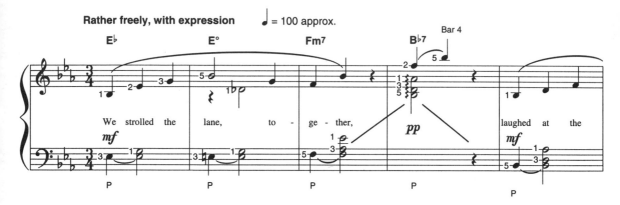

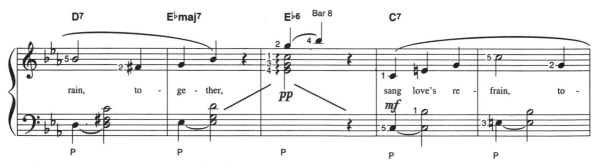

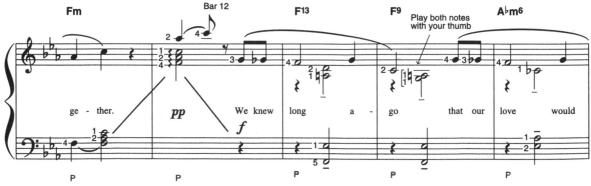

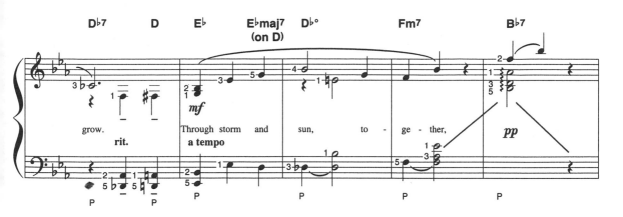

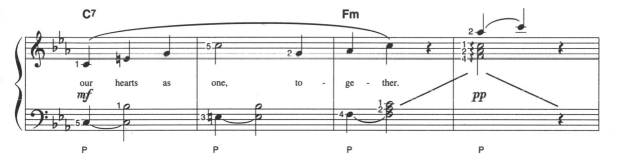

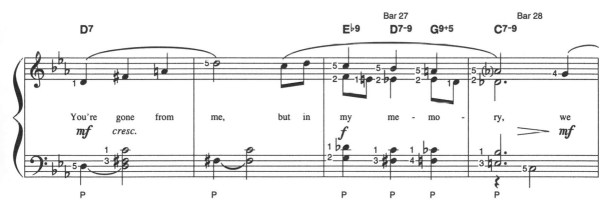

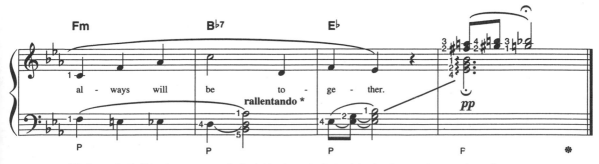

* Rallentando, 'Rall.' for short, means gradually slowing down. A rallentando tends to be more drawn out than a ritenuto.

PHRASING AGAINST

7

Wheels is a playful, cheeky little number, where 'phrasing' is all important.

You will remember from Part Three (page 102) that phrasing is concerned with **how** you play the notes: staccato or legato, with or without an accent, and so on.

In this piece be sure to make the contrast between 'staccato' phrasing in one hand, and 'legato' phrasing in the other. For instance, in Bars 1 and 3, let's hear the 'stabbed' double notes in your left hand contrast with that smooth right hand melody; and in Bar 4, note the first two right hand notes, which are to be played 'staccato', contrasting with the rising left hand figure, which is to be played 'legato'.

WHEELS

Music: Norman Petty. Words: Jimmy Torres & Richard Stephens

(Melody)

la la,   la   la la,   la   la la,   la la   la la.   La

la la,   la   la la,   la   la la,   la   la.

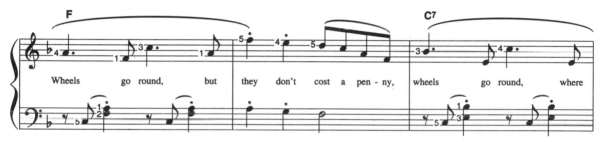

Wheels   go round,   but   they   don't   cost   a   pen - ny,   wheels   go round,   where

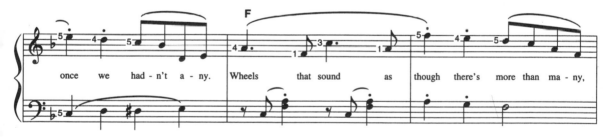

once   we   had - n't   a - ny.   Wheels   that   sound   as   though   there's   more than ma - ny,

fun - ny   lit - tle wheels in - side your   heart.   Fun - ny   lit - tle wheels in - side your   heart.

LEFT HAND JUMPS

8

In the next piece the left hand has to make continuous jumps – down for a low note, up for a chord, and so on. You must develop the capacity to glance quickly down at the keyboard to see where you are going, then back to the music without losing your place.

GYMNOPÉDIE No. 1

By Erik Satie

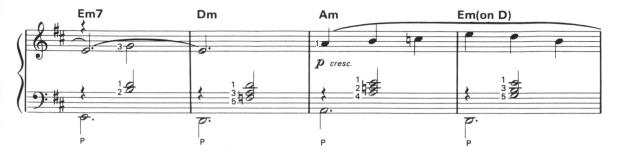

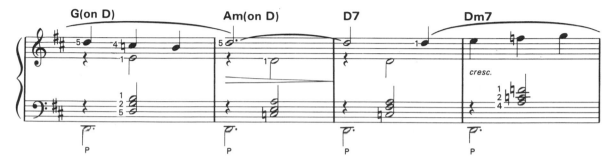

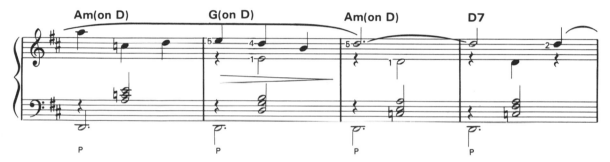

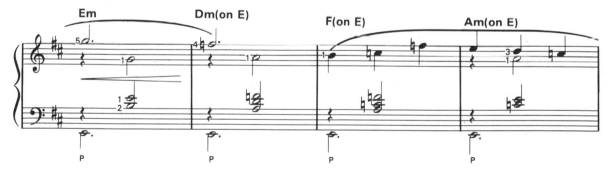

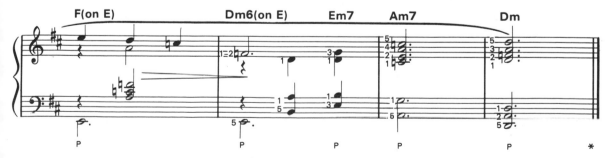

NEW LEFT HAND RHYTHM PATTERN

9

In the first part of *Song For Guy* you will be playing a new left hand rhythm pattern:

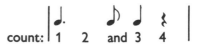

count:

This is similar to the Bossa Nova rhythm pattern first given in Part Four (page 178):

count:

The difference in the *Song For Guy* rhythm is that, having played on the 'and' beat, you hold the note down for the rest of the bar.

SONG FOR GUY
By Elton John

With a gentle rhythm ♩ = 132

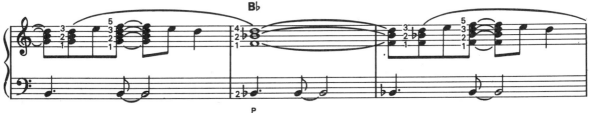

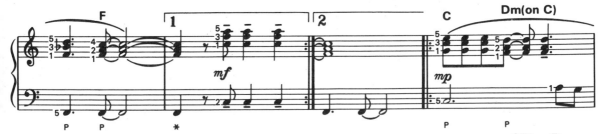

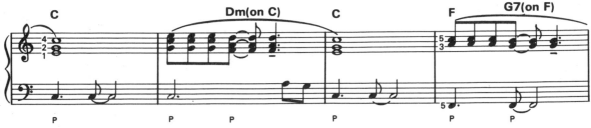

203

KEY OF C MINOR

10

C Minor is the **relative minor** of 'E Flat Major', both keys requiring three flats: B Flat, E Flat, and A Flat:

The accidentals likely to occur in the Key of C Minor are:

B♮ and A♮

The following piece begins in the Key of C Minor and modulates (i.e. changes Key) at the end to E♭ Major (the **relative major**).

Scale/Key of E♭ (Major)

(E♭) F G (A♭) (B♭) C D (E♭)

Scale/Key of C Minor

C D (E♭) F G (A♭) (B♭) C

THE SHADOW OF YOUR SMILE
Words: Paul Francis Webster. Music: Johnny Mandel

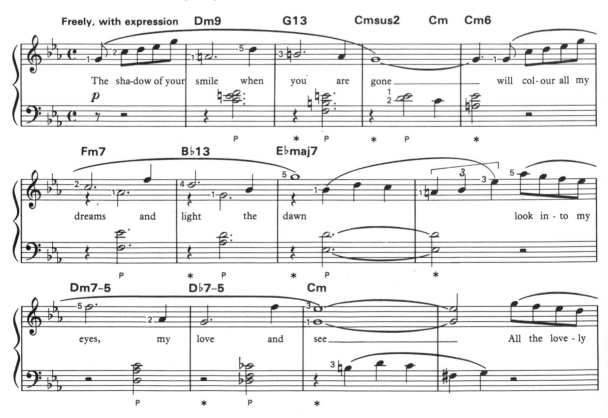

204

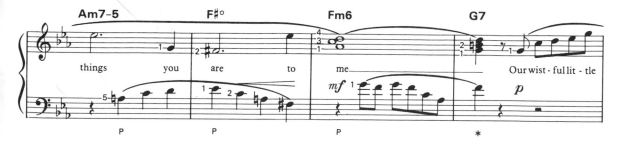

things you are to me

Our wist-ful lit-tle

star was far too high. A tear drop kissed your

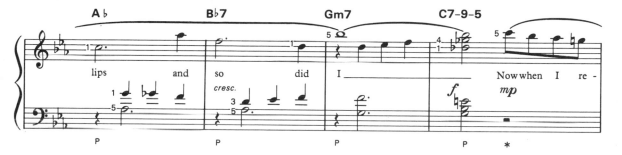

lips and so did I

Now when I re-

mem-ber Spring All the joy that love can bring I will be re-

mem-ber-ing the sha-dow of your smile.

TWO TUNES AT ONCE

In Bars 16-22 of the next piece you play fragments of the main theme of *Can't Smile Without You* with your left hand, while your right hand plays a different theme above it. In other words, you play two tunes at once.

Make your left hand slightly louder than your right hand at this point.

Observe the instruction given at the beginning of the piece: 'with a lilt'.

CAN'T SMILE WITHOUT YOU
Words & Music : Chris Arnold, David Martin & Geoff Morrow

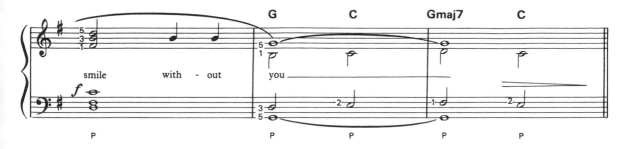

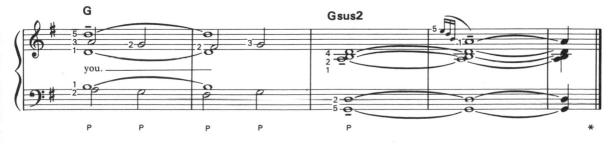

KEY OF A

12

The Key of A (Major) is derived from the Scale of A (Major), which requires three black notes: F Sharp, C Sharp, and G Sharp:

Scale of A

A   B   C♯   D   E   F♯   G♯   A

Pieces using this scale predominantly are said to be in the Key of A.

The Key Signature for the key of A is:

Key of A

F sharp, C sharp, G sharp

When you are in this key you must remember to play all F's, C's, and G's (wherever they might fall on the keyboard) as F Sharps, C Sharps, and G Sharps.

SCALE OF A

13

Before you begin *Prelude in A Major*, by Chopin, play through the Scale of A a few times with your right hand. This is to help you feel the 'shape' of the key. Here's the fingering for two octaves:

Scale of A

Notice that your thumb plays every 'A' and every 'D', except for the top 'A', which is played by your little finger (5), for convenience.

It is always useful to play through the scale of a new key, since it helps teach the fingers where the necessary black notes lie.

PRELUDE IN A MAJOR

By Frederik Chopin

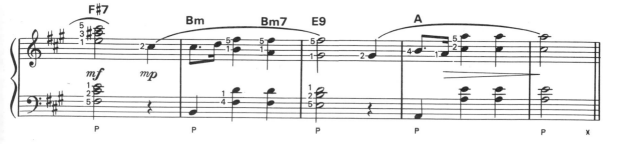

KEY OF A MINOR

14

A Minor is the 'relative minor' key of
C Major, in which there are no sharps or
flats:

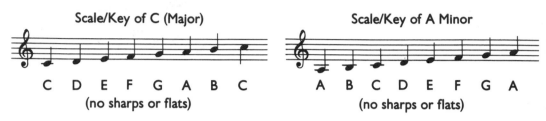

Scale/Key of C (Major)

C D E F G A B C
(no sharps or flats)

Scale/Key of A Minor

A B C D E F G A
(no sharps or flats)

There are two 'accidental' sharps likely to
occur in the Key of A Minor. They are:

G♯ and F♯

As it happens, in *Für Elise* (your piece in
the Key of A Minor), there is another
accidental which keeps appearing:

D♯

This is simply a 'passing note' (see Part
Two, page 70), and has no connection
with the Scale of A Minor.

⅜ TIME

15

Your next piece, Beethoven's *Für Elise*, is
written in ⅜ Time. This means that there
are three quavers (three 'eighth' notes), or
their equivalent, to the bar:

Example

count: 1 2 3 | 1 2 3 | 1 and 2 and 3 and | 1 2 and 3 and | 1 2 3

⅜ Time is usually chosen in preference to
¾ Time when the piece is of a flowing,
running nature, like *Für Elise*.

FÜR ELISE

By: Ludwig Van Beethoven

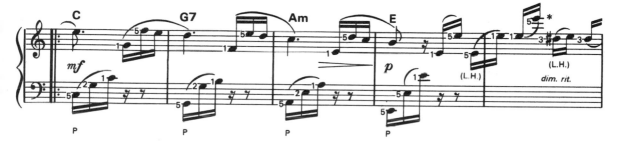

*High E (see p.36)

A STUDY IN ACCIDENTALS

16

Your next piece, *What Are You Doing The Rest Of Your Life?*, is in the key of A Minor. The middle section, however, passes through the keys of A Major, G♭ Major, and F Major, returning again to the key of A Minor for a repeat of the main theme.

This mixture of keys is the reason for the many accidentals (sharps, flats, and naturals, not in the key signature) which you will find in this piece.

WHAT ARE YOU DOING THE REST OF YOUR LIFE?

Words: Alan & Marilyn Bergman. Music: Michel Legrand

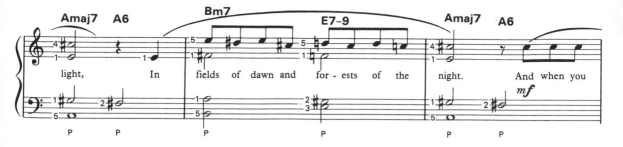

light,   In fields of dawn and for-ests of the night.   And when you

stand be-fore the can-dles on a cake, Oh, let me be the one to hear the si - lent wish you

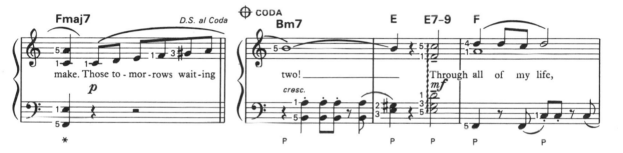

make. Those to - mor-rows wait-ing   two!_____   Through all of my life,

Sum-mer, win-ter, spring and fall of my life,   All I ev - er will re - call of my life, is

all   of   my   life   with   you._____   all of my life with you.

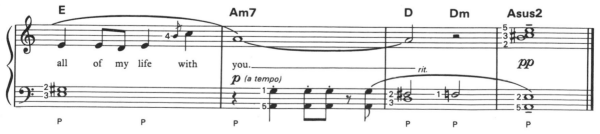

TWO NEW NOTES

High D and E for right hand :

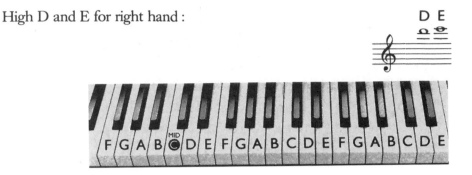

THE ENTERTAINER
By Scott Joplin

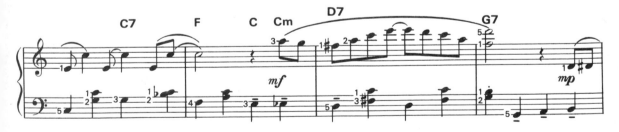

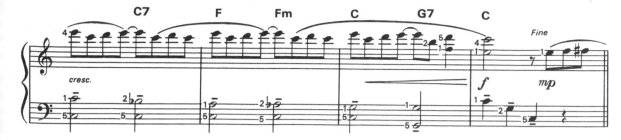

FAST REITERATED NOTES IN THE RIGHT HAND

18

In *With A Little Help From My Friends* there are some fast reiterated 'D's to be played by your right hand (see Bars 9, 11, and 13).

In such passages it is usual to change the finger on each reiterated note to ensure that the note actually plays again. Here are two exercises for you to practise:

Exercise 1

Exercise 2

Keep very close to the keys.
Observe the accents.
Make sure that all the notes play.
Gradually speed up.

WITH A LITTLE HELP FROM MY FRIENDS
Words & Music: John Lennon and Paul McCartney

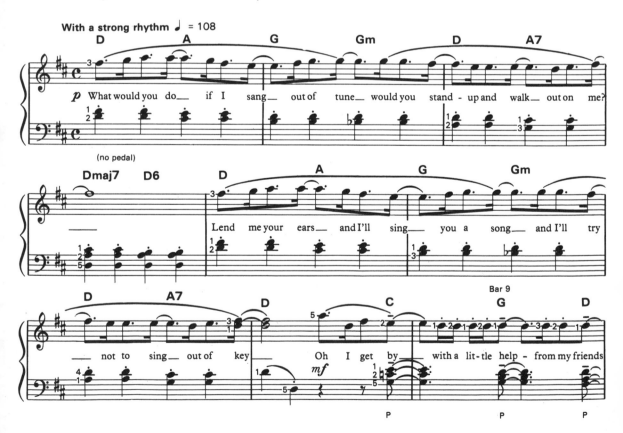

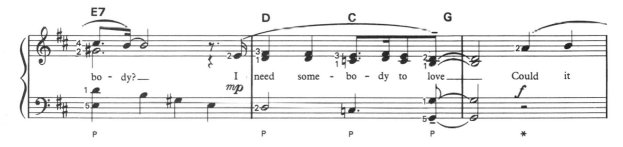

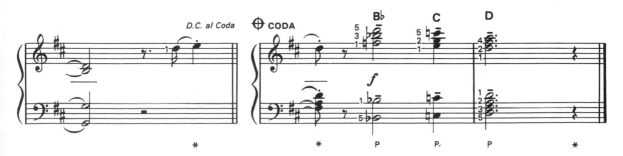

$\frac{3}{2}$ TIME

19

Your next piece, the *Theme From E.T.*, is written in $\frac{3}{2}$ Time. This means that there are three minims (three 'half' notes), or their equivalent, to the bar:

Example

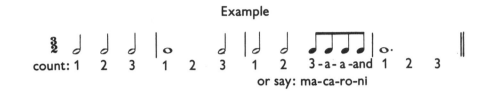

count: 1   2   3   1   2   3   1   2   3-a-a-and 1   2   3

or say: ma-ca-ro-ni

$\frac{3}{2}$ Time is usually chosen in preference to $\frac{3}{4}$ Time when the piece is slow and drawn out, like the *Theme From E.T.*

THEME FROM E.T. (THE EXTRA-TERRESTRIAL)
By John Williams

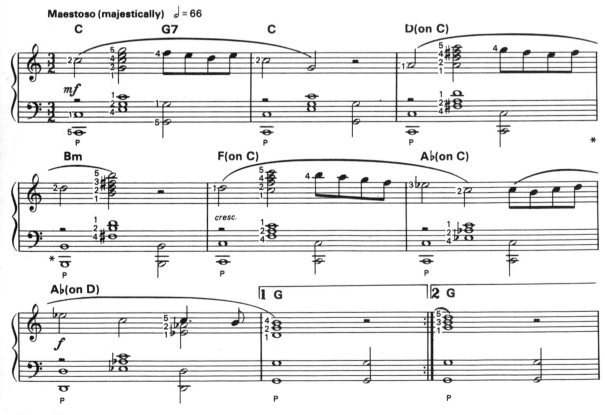

*Low B

218

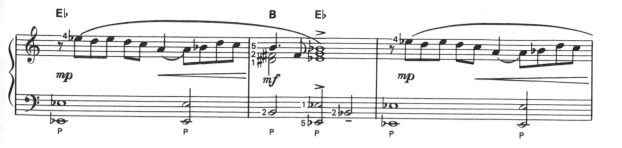

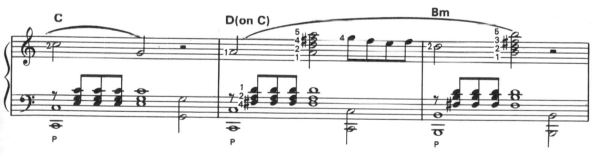

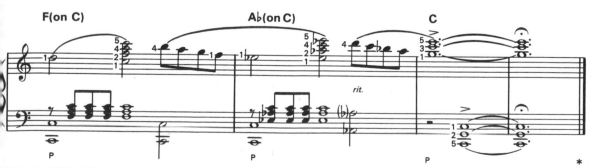

TREMOLO

20

Your next piece: *The Pink Panther Theme,*
is an interesting piece of mood music.
This comic suspense style theme is
greatly enhanced by the use of 'tremolos'.

THE PINK PANTHER THEME

Play the two notes E and B in rapid
succession continuously for a bar and a
half (six crotchet beats).

Use a rolling action of the wrist on your
tremolos rather than finger muscles alone.
Do not hold your wrist too tightly.

THE PINK PANTHER THEME
Words & Music: Henry Mancini

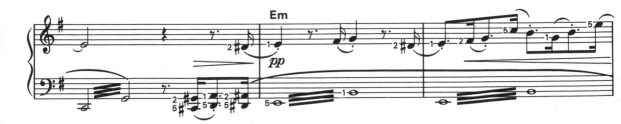

BOTH HANDS HIGH

21

In the next piece, *Music Box Dancer*, both hands play high on the keyboard in order to simulate a musical box. To avoid using a large number of Ledger Lines to express the notes:

● The left hand is written in Treble Clef throughout.

● The right hand is written normally, but is to be played one octave (eight notes) higher than written.
This is expressed: 8va.

Try holding down the Soft Pedal (written: una corda) through this piece: it may improve the musical box effect.

MUSIC BOX DANCER
By Frank Mills

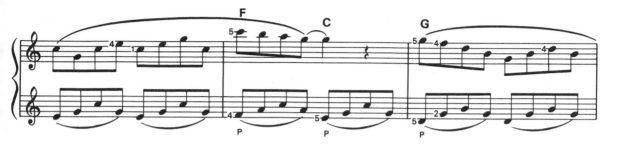

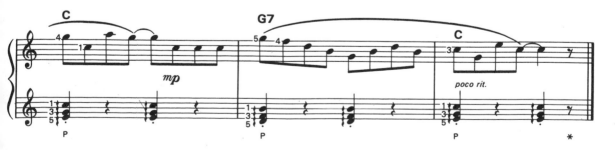

OPEN BROKEN CHORD STYLE FOR LEFT HAND

22 In *Evergreen* your left hand returns again to a 'broken chord' style (see *My Way*, Part Four, page 152, and *Music Box Dancer*, Part Five, page 222). Here in *Evergreen*, however, the chords have been opened up, so the distances you travel will be much greater.

Allow your left wrist to swivel freely from side to side as you encompass the notes.

LAST WORD

You have now reached the end of Part 5 the last book in the Omnibus Edition of 'The Complete Piano Player'. To help you to become a complete all-round player you should continue with 'The Complete Piano Player Style Book'. But you also need to enlarge your repertoire. For this, use 'The Complete Piano Player Songbooks.' They contain fabulous new pieces at all levels, written in the style of 'The Complete Piano Player' books.

In the meantime here is *Evergreen*:

EVERGREEN

Words: Paul Williams. Music: Barbra Streisand

One ____ love that is ____ shared by two
Time ____ we've learned to sail a - bove

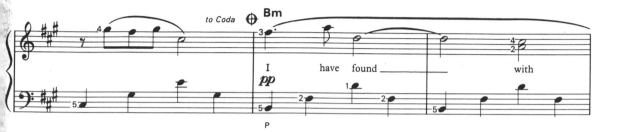

I have found ____ with

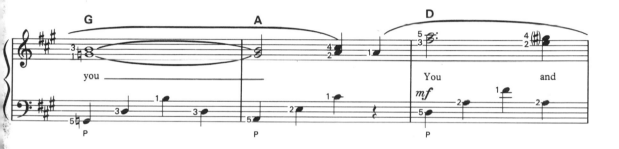

you ____ You and

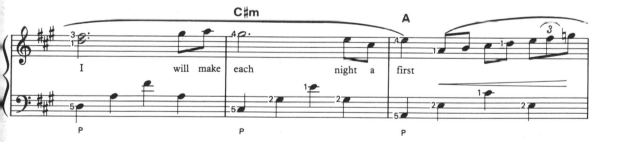

I will make each night a first ____

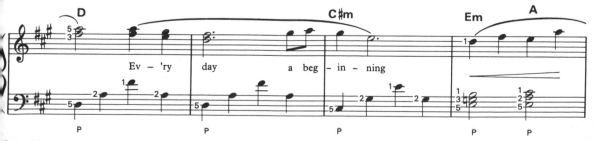

Ev - 'ry day a beg - in - ning

Spir – its rise and their dance is un – re – hearsed.

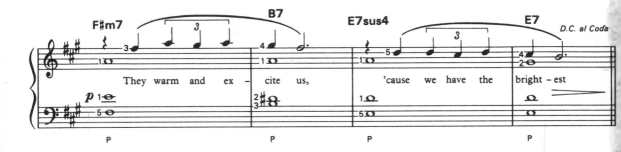

They warm and ex – cite us, 'cause we have the bright – est

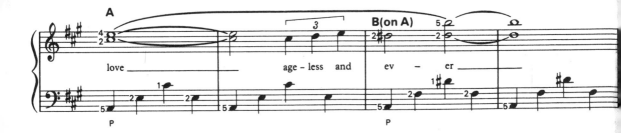

Time _____ won't change the mean – ing of _____ one

love _____ age – less and ev – er _____

Ev – er _____ green. _____